Bring Down the Little Birds

On Mothering, Art, Work, and Everything Else

Carmen Giménez Smith

THE UNIVERSITY OF ARIZONA PRESS

TUCSON

The University of Arizona Press
© 2010 Carmen Giménez Smith
All rights reserved

www.uapress.arizona.edu

Library of Congress Cataloging-in-Publication Data
Giménez Smith, Carmen, 1971–
    Bring down the little birds / Carmen Giménez Smith.
        p. cm.—(Camino del sol)
    ISBN 978-0-8165-2869-1 (pbk. : alk. paper)
    I. Title.
    PS3607.I45215B75 2010
    811'.6—dc22

                                                    2010003227

Publication of this book is made possible in part by the proceeds of a
permanent endowment created with the assistance of a Challenge Grant
from the National Endowment for the Humanities, a federal agency.

Manufactured in the United States of America on acid-free, archival-
quality paper containing a minimum of 30% post-consumer waste and
processed chlorine free.

15   14   13   12   11   10   6   5   4   3   2   1

for Yolanda Noemi Roselló

and Sofia Aurora Smith

Bring Down the Little Birds

I daydream that I'm thirteen sitting in an attic in my mother's wedding dress. I discover a notebook, in it the evidence of my mother's secret life. I write notes from her book into mine, which is, years later, discovered by my son.

From my mother's imaginary notebook: sketch of dancer, sketch of cabaret singer. *I engage in gluttony and wild behavior.*

I think we are on the track of a lost novelist, a suppressed poet.

From my notebook: *A secret is a curse. I was picked from the throngs with nothing to show.*

I wonder if my children will one day discover my secret life? Will they read the notebooks in my study? Will they care?

Because I cared little for my mother's interior, it didn't exist for me. My mother couldn't be a mystery. . . . She was only a mystery when I needed one for the story I made of my life.

From her notebook, the one I've imagined for her: *I would have liked to have been a dancer, I would have liked to have been a singer.* So many verbs away from herself. I would have liked to have known her better, but I was too occupied pulling her out of herself. Now the tables are turned—it's a brand new table.

From my notebook: *The bud of a baby inside me.*

My mother says that motherhood is never going to the bathroom alone again.

Two weeks ago my mother had tests performed on her, the beginning of an explanation. How her memory is leaking out of her, why so much weakness in her hands and in her mind.

In my mother's big, empty house in California, she holds her hands up to the light to see how living has deformed her. She had always been young, and then, suddenly, she was old. *Aging motherhoods you.* She loathes her job selling vacuum cleaners six days a week and commuting three hours a day. She says to herself, to me, matter-of-factly: *It's the way it is.*

Mother: matter, wood, the source.

The word *mother*, where it came from. The word *mama* existing in so many languages. Or is it all languages? Mother, roots that fix me to the earth. Umbilical tethers. *Matrices,* then *cicatriz* . . . Spanish for *scar.* Motherhood = scar. The stretch marks on the skin over my hips, that cradle they make. Matrices like the pith of an orange, ragged and juicy.

Saying the word *mother* and feeling mealymouthed—a derogatory word.

I watch my son's gestures and wonder what part he's acting out: my husband's or mine? Can this really be? Our children? Our lineage?

The percentages.

I walk out of the English Department office like my mother: hurried, distracted, glasses half falling off.

This morning, I said good-bye to my son so hastily. Regret takes over in the car. Just the day before I so wished to have a day away from him.

Children have everything of someone else's.

*   *   *

I live in the desert, a house nestled low in a New Mexican valley. I walk the dog early, like all my neighbors, and I look at them closely, an attempt to determine motherhood-proficiency by the shape of their faces. Some of them mothers themselves; some someday mothers; some disdaining motherhood now and some forever.

I feel not noticed, invisible cloak of mother. I want the gaze, the sexual one from before . . . but the small lump of this second pregnancy precludes it.

Second pregnancy. To have a son, to have a daughter: two different roads. If I have a daughter, she joins me for good. If I have a daughter, I will never say I am fat. I will tell her I had lots of good, healthy sex when I was old enough, when I was in love. It somehow doesn't matter with a son. He's not watching me in this way. Or perhaps he is, perhaps I'm ruining him a little.

The lives of my students and their mothers' parts in them. Parties and lazily reading magazines in their lovers' beds. They know what's fashionable these days. Jeans exposing unrazed bellies. Complicated sweaters that would belie breast-feeding.

And what do their mothers know of their lives?

*　　*　　*

To crave is a symptom of pregnancy. It's a cavernous hunger. I eat constantly, although what grows in me will only be eight pounds. I have twenty percent more blood now. I thicken it with fat plums, yeasty breads.

When my son was first born, his hungry, desperate, half-blind eyes found me through my voice or smell alone—both fascinating and repulsive to me. That he was so animal. Or that the exchange was so instinctual: a pig rooting in mud for his food. I called him Piggy for weeks.

Feeding him left me tired and sore. My nipples cracked. I treated them with lanolin, sheep oil. This is a farm thing. . . . Pig, sheep, cow.

I revealed my body wearily. His greed was contagious: it began to look like love. His head nestled in my chest like his father's. I stroked his downy hair, like his father's.

My body suddenly belonged to the world. In a restaurant, I felt the air of exposure, the stare of strangers as my son rooted noisily against me—*and I relished it.*

I show pictures of my son to anyone who asks anything about me. Yes, I'm *that* mother.

It's a collision of desires, nothing more.

*   *   *

During my first pregnancy, I read books that described the particulars of every week. I read them so eagerly that I still know them by heart. . . . This week the baby inside me is the size of a small mouse.

During this second pregnancy, I want a different book—the one that tells of my life, its outcomes, how to be prepared. *This week you will feel ambivalence about being pregnant because you're angry about not having time to yourself. This hour will move much too slowly when you're alone with your son and you just don't want to play with Buzz Lightyear. Your son will develop a weird thing about the feathers from the comforter and there's nothing you can do about that . . . good luck with that one!*

*   *   *

I hear of other writers my age with children, but I don't know them and they don't know me.

I have a list of questions to ask. Or I think I do. But I don't know how to ask or don't have the words for my questions. I want to know another mother made imperfect by her desire for herself, but how do you ask that? I want her there, some other mother. I want to know that my anxiety is *typical.*

In my office at work, I scour the Internet for discussion boards. Kinship, kinship . . . but I can't bear the misspellings of Kutemom13. I should be grading papers, writing letters of recommendation. . . . Instead I am trying to have a conversation about: To be two and do what? Mother and write, mother and work, mother and _____.

I bring work home when it doesn't get done at work, nurse my son to sleep, only to slip away and play catch-up.

As an undergraduate I met Joyce Carol Oates when she gave a reading at my school. I asked her the question I had always imagined asking her: *Joyce Carol Oates, how do you write so much?*

She had a schedule, she told me. Run in the morning, write for four hours. Run in the afternoon, write for four hours.

Ah, I thought to myself. No children.

Writers with children writing about children.

Writers afraid to write too much about their children because they still want to inhabit an adult world.

Writers whose children write about their parents' lives, about making their own meals, helping mimeo their mothers' literary magazines, all those sultry bohemian hot-tub parties.

Writers with more than one child. Flaubert writing of a woman's discontent while his own mother minded her dead daughter's daughter. Writers with no children, prolific ones. Prolific writers with many children. Leo Tolstoy. Charles Dickens. Writers with wives.

Women writers with many children. Marie Ponsot. Lucille Clifton. *As I stand here ironing.*

All the women writers without children.

Which is it: Selfish Mother or Selfless Mother? Is this the only choice?

Motherhood as conundrum. . . . What would *Erma Bombeck* do?

Why I became a writer: To write my mother's way out of the tedium.

*   *   *

My husband writes a short story in which a young protagonist discovers a cache of books filled with his ailing mother's marginalia. The story is about a son wanting to know his mother. This is a truth for all of us.

And how do we write the mother with nuance? Art has trouble with the contradictions. We want to punish our mothers for what we felt got left out.

In my husband's story, a map of the mother, messages she leaves for him to discover. When reading a book, everything I read returns me to my son, how he might see it, how he might better understand it, how I could better help him understand how I see it. I make notes on the page—just in case.

My friend, a male poet, says that poets are ruined when they have children. So maybe I want to ask, *Is this your anxiety too?* I know lots of mothers. Mothers who mother and rock climb, mothers who mother and midwife. But writing further complicates the idea of how one makes things in the world, other things. Words, thoughts, language. I'm talking about language.

When I was first pregnant and not writing, friends told me it was okay because I was *creating life,* that the fire of writing poetry was being *redistributed.* That fire which felt like a stroke-afflicted arm. *In what furnace? In what brain?* I received their suggestions indubitably and grew a son in me. I couldn't write: my fire had been rerouted. I imagined that this meant my son would be born filled with all my unwritten parturient poems.

Anything I try to write: fraught with motherhood. I don't want to be that sentimental mother, but I just can't help it. *A poem that is being written, even if it looks like a subject.*

From my mother's imaginary notebook: *Today I left everything behind for a day and went to the ocean. I threw my apron in the water.*

*   *   *

My son has words for the world now. *Wish* for fish. *Earth. Moon. Doggie.* His vocabulary is all element, all noun. The entire world belongs to him. I dream that he tells me what he sees through the window, using a pretty good metaphor. That feels insincere. I investigate his lexicon. The natural world and the world of prohibition: *no-no, uh-oh.* Then we're back to want. *Meat. Milk.* It's all want, really, this acquisition of language. He understands what *me* means, although when I ask him who he is, he says, *Mom.* Because we are the same thing.

*   *   *

This semester the department assigned me a children's literature class. Is this the motherhood ghetto of academia?

I make plans to subvert it. And not just the curriculum—my motherhood as well.

Sometimes I am nothing but my work. Mothering diffuses me into a mist and work clarifies the margins.

The world of books was once my sole priority. I cut school to read. I didn't go to parties and concerts to read. Didn't work, didn't fall in love because of books. Today my son plants himself in front of the book I'm reading and, despite my best efforts, I can't see through him to the page.

For class, a discussion with students about Snow White and her stepmother. I tell them that this might be a story about a daughter and her natural mother.

So many women in the room . . . we talk about being daughters, our Snow White days. My mother's vanity flashes in the room. Her stiletto heels, her gold-threaded sweaters.

Another way in which she was a mystery: For whom was she always dressing up?

A student reads her response aloud about beauty. *Some people tell me I am beautiful but I don't see it, or struggle with what they mean. Do they mean beautiful on the outside? Because that's so fleeting and desirable. Or beautiful inside? Because that matters less.*

To be a beautiful protagonist. Envy eats my heart: I am the wicked mother. Once I wanted nothing more than austerity. I ask my husband to tell me what I am. He offers me reassuring abstractions that tell me absolutely nothing about my face.

I'm a good mother and a good poet, but I want a great ass and fabulous hair.

I admit to my class that I once loathed my mother because I thought I was beautiful and she was not. She embarrassed me because she wasn't young, she wasn't fresh.

Now I am a mother of one, another on the way. I spent my beauty on folly. Now I'm past the mirror.

I thought my mother wanted to eat me alive, two women in a house with only one mirror to share.

One student suggests that the wicked stepmother is going through menopause.

I ask them to inhabit that mother for a moment, to imagine how the mirror might make them crazy.

We look at the end of Snow White, the new cruelness. The mother dancing herself to death for the daughter's satisfaction.

Our mothers chase us through the woods and bring us back, only to finally eat us.

Some women tell about reading the story to their daughters. I wonder about doing the same someday. There'll be perversity in that reading to her: she will be my mirror, I hers. I'll scry the mirror to find her, wherever she might be.

*   *   *

I remember some ways in which my mother was a mystery to me. She never cried, for example, maybe once or twice. So disarming, I cry all the time. . . . How else?

About being a mother she taught me one could give it, then take it away, depending. . . .

Once, on a very cold day in Maryland, where we briefly lived—we always lived briefly—my brother and I came home from school, and my mother had a hot bath ready for us. She took off our clothes, put us in the tub that both warmed and stung. Then she wrapped us in towels and blankets, took us to our rooms, helped us into pajamas, recently warmed in the dryer. She tucked us into her bed. We ate tomato soup on trays. A pair of heirs, a series of warmings.

I remember the entitlement I felt. My mother's love was no privilege. This was her gift to my brother and me.

Or: A series of warnings?

What could she have been doing instead of warming us? What could I have been doing but eagerly accepting that warmth?

*   *   *

My son's small proficiencies, each one a relief to me, each one signaling independence. And each signaling growing complexity. *Mama, my big big sad.*

Somewhere behind the pleasure my son gives me is my mother, who, without my noticing, has grown past the age of thirty-five, the age I always thought right for her, maybe the last time I asked her age. She's sixty now, the age my grandmother was the last time I asked her age, the age at which she is forever frozen in my mind.

Two paths that cross and diverge. I look for pockets of time while my son learns that plants are living things not to be shredded haphazardly. Motherhood has burned new paths in me. Routes replaced with thornier ones.

I learn to tolerate and negotiate phone calls with my mother. She asks the same questions again and again. Is she listening? I answer as if each question has been asked for the first time. It wears on me, but I have to do it. For my mother's sake. No, for mine. *For my sake and for all our sakes.*

While she talks, my son pulls on my legs, insisting that I hold him. I look around my kitchen: the chipped Formica counter I finger as my mother complains, the cracking walls. I wash the dishes at a window through which I lament the dying basil. He clings to me, he clings and clings. I would politely ask him to comprehend my grown-woman, adult conundrum of having a mother with tenuous health. I think to mute the phone. To my son, death is not yet an abstraction.

When I get tired of being touched, of holding and answering, I retreat into my interior, a place of which I can barely speak because it fills me with shame to want to be away. Because if I speak of it, if I force words upon it, it will immediately become ordinary.

Mother Worn Down to the Bone from Touching.

This retreat is an island. A cabana on a beach, a bar where *one can still smoke cigarettes*. The music's really, really loud. It's Boards of Canada, it's Aphex Twin, all and everything I need.

And when are you coming? my mother asks. *And the boy, how is he?* my mother asks. *And the husband?* my mother asks.

Then I asked, *Why?* Now I ask, *How?*

How did you find time to do the dishes? How does anyone turn mothering into writing? Turn mothering into anything other than mothering? And why would one want to, besides?

I think I know the answers. I don't want to know the answers. They've got something to do with giving up, giving in, giving over. But in which direction? Ah, there's the rub.

*   *   *

When I found out I was pregnant for the second time, I wrestled with telling the chair of my department, a woman with no children. I was afraid of how being pregnant again would look to the world of work. Weak, unfocused. Divided. *Mommy.*

I was afraid of the male colleague who looked through me as if I were a ghost, ghostmother. As if to ask, *Shouldn't you be at home?*

Mama, manna, motor, motherfucker. We're surrounded. *Mom* is the lull of water. It's a kiss. *Mama* mimics the smacking of a baby's lips onto her mother's breast. *Mama* is a mouth clamp twice.

The body stirs. The body *stirs* with pregnancy.

I try to explain the timeline of pregnancy to my boss. I think to say, *I feel as if I am floating on air but also fraught with arrows,* but of course I end up telling her it will be very easy to balance work and family. I efface the rigors of the last weeks of pregnancy, guarantee that I will stop working for one, two weeks at most.

I have no choice. I am a pregnant woman in the world of work. I will not allow pregnancy to be my excuse.

My body remembers, it gives in. I never wanted a *woman's body,* but that's what I got. I want that lean body I had three years ago, before I was pregnant with my son—those legs! that ass!—not the lumpy Venus body from art history class. My son sits on my hip like it's a perfectly proportioned perch . . . and still, somehow, there's going to be room for one more?

My son is finally venturing out into the world, and here another one comes, venturing in.

Both a thrill and a sorrow.

Becoming a mother, being a mother makes me feel taller, larger . . . I've got a bustling bottom. In a childbirth class, one of our midwives, Kamy, asks the couples in attendance to draw pictures of the animal they imagine the laboring mother to be. I draw a cow with a big, round middle, tiny legs. My husband draws a bear.

These days, if I wanted to—and yes, I want to—I could knock down skinny, childless women with my bottom. My husband says he loves it, my big butt, but I know he's lying.

*   *   *

I call my friend who has a daughter one year older than my son and a pregnancy a few months further along than mine. We talk about the way our bodies are changing this time. She's having another cesarean, I'm having another home birth, and in this difference, in all our differences, we somehow find comfort. Like we lack a little conviction in our choice until it's countered by another's opposite choice—and then suddenly we really like our choice! I try to convince her to breast-feed, but I know she won't.

Or I assume she won't: motherhood as a form of piety. I talk a lot about the piety of the mothers I hear talking at the park, yet I'm just as pious. I cringe when, sitting at a doctor's office, I see a woman give her son fiery hot Cheetos.

The things I won't do as mother, the things I will. What I concede, what I cling to. . . . What I cling to desperately.

That this piety, misplaced—that this piety, sublimated—becomes a fantasy of mothering the world. If I had to do it my way, if I could show people how it's done . . . with my bustling bottom. Worst or best, no matter: I am the mother of the world.

We talk about how we're raising our children, and I find myself lying a bit: about what my son eats, about how much TV he watches, about how my husband and I are(n't) getting along.

My friend lies, too—or so I hope—because from where I sit listening, her life sounds marvelous, velvety smooth.

How do I want the world to see me as mother? How will it? Angry Mother. Saintly Mother. The Mother Who Overcompensates. The Clumsy Mother. The Disorganized Mother. The Chronically Late Mother. The Distant Mother.

A Hundred Therapy Sessions Worth of Mother. The Best Friend Mother.

*   *   *

When my son was a newborn, he twitched in his sleep; it terrified me, I couldn't speak of it. I was afraid all the drugs I'd once consumed had damaged him preemptively. I pored over the Internet: "previous drug use" +pregnancy. Clearing the search history from the computer.

There was a time I didn't live like a mother. Whatever that meant at the time.

*   *   *

Because when I was a child my mother could never locate scissors or Band-Aids, I fill the drawers of my house with such things. My mother worked three jobs. She came home, worked more. Scissors and Band-Aids necessarily fell by the wayside.

She worked as a housekeeper and a waitress. She worked in hotels and restaurants and lodges. She sold Mary Kay and Avon and vacuum cleaners. All so I wouldn't have to.

How many hours, exactly, have I spent looking for scissors?

My children will fill their drawers with _____ and _____.

My mother could never remember to sign permission slips. A public television station films my class playing on the playground; I stay inside and play connect-the-dots for two hours.

Instead, she taught us how to do a scarf dance indigenous to Peru. She watched Katharine Hepburn movies with us late into the night. She once sewed me a satin Pierrot costume.

There are no combs to be spoken of in this house, no matter how long I spend looking for the comb I know we own.

When I was six, my mother told my brother and me that we were twins separated from birth by several months. She told me the birthmark on my belly was the eclipsed moon burning my skin. A schoolteacher explained, gently, that this could not possibly be true.

My mother unwove the weave of fairy tales to suit her pragmatism: Cinderella leaving to start a dry-cleaning business.

Misled by my mother, I think of the quick-on-her-footedness of it, keeping me out of her life, keeping me interested in mine. Yet another way she is and was a mystery.

This was her poetry. Her poems, her so many mysteries.

I once thought it would be easy to look back on how I was mothered, to classify it, categorize it, but it's not so easy at all. What I once thought of as *bad mothering* I now understand as the condition consequent to the tedium of the act, the process.

I hear it in myself, my voice at bedtime, getting ready for school. I'm yelling outside of my sense.

I have a friend who won't forgive his mother; it's because he isn't a mother. I wish upon him motherhood, sadistically, soulfully—I wish for him a comprehension of its vastness.

I yell, use the TV for respite . . . I jerk my son's writhing body still in the car seat. I eat Brie when I'm pregnant, drink a mojito to celebrate a birthday. I let him cry or fall. I fail, I fail.

Mother is heavy matter, lead. Weighed down with my son in my arms, groceries, a diaper bag, the baby inside me. I am bound to this earth by downward momentum.

*   *   *

Yet another way my mother was a mystery: her ceaseless energy. Did she ever stop? She was awake when I went to bed, she woke me in the mornings. She was the shoemaker's elf, remaking the house each night. We lived in a dozen or more houses together, a forever peripatetic life she worked so hard to stabilize. I don't remember a single home ever being even half-made.

The once and only time I remember seeing my mother in bed was after she gave birth to my sister. My grandmother brought her tea. My grandmother pushed her back down onto the bed when my mother insisted on getting up.

She never complained. Her burdens—so many—are inaccessible to me. She makes light of them, jokes of them, to conceal her suffering. Is this mothering?

*   *   *

My husband and I have a date. We take our son to my father-in-law's and we go back home to have sex. Afterward we talk about our son. Sometimes our conversations circle back to art or to money, but mostly we relish in our son's particulars. Both our bodies—my husband's and mine—colonized by this insistent presence. I wander the halls of our house: the hollowness of my son's absence is exquisite.

Or we wait until my son is sleeping to make love; he sleeps on the far end of the bed. Sometimes he wakes up: he looks on patiently; or through the movement of the bed, he's rocked back to sleep. My husband and I sit together— we talk about him, his face, his hands. The way his fingernails fit wide over his fingers, the slenderness of his knees. . . . And how is it there is another baby inside me with a different face, different hands, fingernails and knees? Will her birth improve our sex life if my husband and I have two sets of postcoital particulars in which to revel?

Our other midwife, Tawnya, praises our house. It doesn't look overrun by childhood, she says. But to me nothing could be further from the truth. It's been made bare and things have been hidden on account of my son's curious hands; I've winnowed away my precious belongings and set them high up on a shelf.

My son's room is beautiful, like a movie set. We painted it the blue I found after staring at paint chips for an hour at Home Depot. I had my husband install a light fixture shaped like a sun. I want his room to feel like Childhood, and I want my hand in that.

Our bedroom is unpainted, like a monk's chamber. Our bed is stained with breast milk and urine. This is where we sleep. Somehow, we're fine with that.

*   *   *

My friends ask me if my mother has a boyfriend. Never. Absolutely not. It piques their interest. My parents divorced for twenty years and my mother never dated?

No. No way. Hell no.

I ask her about actors in movies in order to get a sense of what she might . . . want. Do you like Banderas or Clooney? *Too dark,* she says of both.

Luce Irigaray says that in order for us to be liberated, we must liberate our mother's sexuality. Clearly, this is too distasteful to me.

My mother's wildly sexual life? Nights to herself? I wonder about having nights to myself. What I think about doing, pure self-indulgence: *Muscles better and nerves more.* Could she ever? No, no, no, no.

Surely there is such a thing as the total absence of desire. And if not, is it something I contrive in order to not feel pity for my mother? Desirous, I would not recognize her.

A friend asks, *Have you ever talked to her about it?* and I answer, *Hell to the no.*

Better alone than in bad company, my mother says, regarding remarriage. Desire = bad company.

I attempt to write poems about my mother's desire, but they always become poems about loneliness. Or poems about my own desires.

Maybe she felt it her responsibility to abandon sexuality for her children's sake. That's the answer I live with, my rationalization. *Who's ever been naked?* . . . not my mother.

From my mother's notebook: *He loves my crooked pinkie and that my hair smells of peaches.* From mine: *I can hardly bear it.*

My mother's body, shorter, wider. All of a sudden we wear the same size shoe. Her body trying to tell something to mine.

Hija, she says on the phone. *Don't grow old.*

*   *   *

When I was eleven, we moved to San Jose, California, right next door to the Catastrophic Mother. I befriended her daughter in order to relish in her mother's disasters. The mother would sit on the peeling picnic bench in their backyard, smoking cigarettes and talking on the phone, the long, kinked cord stretched all the way from the kitchen. I half-listened to her daughter; my attention was riveted on this mother-not-so-mother. It seemed that her life entertained her, the way she described it: *My mom had to send me money Western Union and it's already spent every penny but that's it because my dad's an A-S-S hole and I bought red shoes yesterday finally have a date tonight don't know about the kid I guess either TV or her friend's house.*

     The Catastrophic Mother's house smelled of cigarettes; I left my coat on the front porch. The laundry piled on the couch . . . the Catastrophic Mother would push it all to the floor so that her daughter and I could watch MTV with her, practice dance moves. Catastrophic Mother was going to go to college, going to be a beautician, training to be a chef, someday sell real estate in Vegas. *Can you imagine me as an actress?* she asked. Beds always unmade. Dishes with encrusted macaroni and cigarette wrappers.

     Her desire was clear to me even as a child. I had never seen *sexual desire* in a mother. She even smelled like it: perfume and sweat. Their house made me feel prudish and prissy and my mother's rules embarrassed me.

*   *   *

After a second pregnancy, I am *multiparous*. Been there, done that. The first time, I feel like a pioneer; the second, a sheep.

Yesterday I called my son *brother*. Brother to the lump in me. I hope he is delighted about the baby, and I hope his delight becomes contagious. A book about second pregnancy suggests resignation: *You may not be as excited as the first time around.*

You'll show sooner, feel more tired.

My pregnancy softens my edges in the classroom. Pros and cons. It protects me from the students' discontent about their grades and assignments, but it makes them see me as motherly.

What *motherly* means: that I'll coddle, that I'll coo.

Is this what I thought? Is this what I think?

The number of my female professor colleagues who have children: two (2).

*   *   *

I get migraines this time around. Debilitated by hormones, I cringe under a blanket while my son shrieks *Chi-Chi! Chi-Chi!* I want to disappear, become vapor, but only if my husband holds my son while I vaporize. When I stand up, I list to the side. I am carried to the car. Some doctor feeds me pills that make us all—mother, toddler, fetus—sleepy. I wake up several times in the night to make sure everyone is still breathing.

The migraines become small vacations. *No, not tonight. I've got a headache.*

*   *   *

When frustrated with us, my mother would say, *Me sacan canas verdes.* Green grayhairs.

Her mother died in childbirth, fifth pregnancy. A Victorian novel set in Lima, Peru. My mother was her mother's favorite. Her mother kept mine inside, making her rice pudding, singing her songs, while her three sisters played outside.

When my mother left home that morning, her mother lay in the bed, groggy but smiling. Old hat, fifth baby. She kissed my mother and said, *Next time I see you, you'll have a new brother or sister.* The midwife was sent for, and the housekeeper brought pillows to put under my mother's mother's head.

When she tells the story, my mother stretches it out, squeezes every last ounce of narration from it because it has the shortest and longest ending of any story my mother knows.

The little bit of mother she had spread thin over all her life. I seldom ask her about her mother because of what I imagine the size of that wound to be, and how I imagine the wound of my own mother's death, suddenly imminent in my world, will be like in me.

I have often imagined my young mother at school that day, eagerly awaiting a new brother or sister to hold in her arms. And then the *then.*

*   *   *

My husband decides on a name for a girl. He is eager for a daughter. Fatherhood came to him suddenly, unexpectedly, and so he is enthusiastic that this time we have more agency . . . a name. When I was first pregnant with our son, we weren't sure what to do. I promised him he would have time to write, and now we fight endlessly about this broken promise.

He's the father who curls around his son, whose son finds comfort in him just as he does his mother. He's the father who masters the heart monitor at the first prenatal.

It's not the name I chose, but it's a good name. She will be lovely and dark with a name like this. She will wear beads in her hair and lead a protest for a hopeless and noble cause. She will have boyfriends that play in bands and major in engineering. Then she will pair off with one of them. She will have children right away. They will be wild and well loved. She will paint portraits for a living. She will call her father *Daddy* until the end. It's a name I might have had.

Her middle name: the same as mother's mother's.

*   *   *

Sixteen weeks and we are back and forth and back and forth on the decision to take the test that tells you whether or not you will have a baby with its insides on the outside. Our midwives don't approve. They ask, *What would you do?* My husband and I know, but we don't say. We would travel to the nearest clinic three somber hours away to *take care of it,* because we . . .

Our hesitations must become euphemisms. Awful and small in the face of our selfishness, we take the test anyway.

Two kids, two kids. I repeat the thought over and over, so many failed attempts to allay its banality. The supermarket-meltdown-quality of it. The minivan-beans-and-franks of it. The endless-laundry-Disney-DVD-collection of it.

The eating-at-the-McDonald's-inside-the-Walmart of it.

Perhaps if we moved to Paris it would be cosmopolitan and edgy. It would be raising two children *abroad.*

*   *   *

Every morning seems like every other morning: same dishes, same sink, laundry basket overflowing with the same dirty clothes. *Family,* from the Latin, *familia:* household servants.

In alone time I remember pre-motherhood alone time, how vast and useless it was. Today I get two and a half hours in which to work. I edit an essay and read the news. I make neat piles of papers on my desk and feel deeply satisfied when I leave my office to pick up my son from the babysitter's.

Then I guilt-power-mother him. This is extreme mothering: six books, play cars, play guys, watch *Finding Nemo* for the nth time.

Time allotted in small, slightly melted squares. Same way I take my chocolate.

I want to be with him. I don't want to be with him.

Being without him is still being with him, in my mind.

My son pounds at my locked door, while the babysitter wearily encourages him to come outside and play. The tug, it's a gravitational pull toward the largest object in the world: my son's closed fist. I want. I want. I want so much to stop what I'm doing, I want so much to not stop what I'm doing.

I want so much.

A book being written, a meter ticking. *I get positively angry with the impertinence of it and the everlastingness.*

Round-trip drive to my office at school. Tick tock. This will be costly. It wasn't before. Tick tock. The calculus I do takes three minutes from the writing. Tick tock. Tick tock. Tick tock.

I am compelled to continue writing as I am compelled to continue working as I am compelled to hold my son to my body when he is hot with fever.

One of my mysteries when he's grown, the goings-on behind that closed door. *What the hell is she building in there?*

Or, likely, he'll have constructed his own narrative, one beginning on my side of a door and ending in a feeling of lack and abandonment on his.

*   *   *

One morning in bed, I'm telling him the world and he's telling it back. We go through the inventory of a desert landscape through the windows: the ocotillo that lays a shadow on our bed at night, the rabbit we call *pinecone*, the century plant's open palms. He asks, concerned, after the rabbit's wife.

What's that, Mama?

That's a _____.
Why, Mama, why?

I had always thought a child was defined, demarcated, by his parents; but now, not so much: sometimes he is a stranger, nothing at all like his father or me.

At 21 months, his hair is beginning to curl. He's really, really into the moon.

No difference yet between the known and the unknown. The world must be simplified.

The silly, unanswerable questions rolling and rolling off his tongue. *Why don't trains have mommies?*

His curiosity exceeds my capacity for its assuagement. *Where does wind come from? Which star is that? What's the biggest number of all time?* At a certain point, my proficiency as his guide in the world plummets—I don't understand enough of it.

But also I want him to know what I know, to download what I know into his little brain and body. I want him to have that as a vaccination against grief. I imagine the impossible labor of instilling morality, awareness and compassion. I feel like too small a fount because I have been such a series of errors.

Why is light in the lamp? What do rabbits drink?

I want to tear his *whys* into little pieces. Now I can barely stand the questions. They begin to *anger* me: Where does this rage come from? Was I born with it, taught it, a bit of both? *You think your temper is the worst in the world, but mine used to be just like it.*

My mother was often short with us: extravagant with both her love and rage. She hit me. She thought it would make me *right.* I struggle with what comes instead of the spank, like there's a word on the tip of my tongue, an urge. A syllogism: All spanking is damaging; I was spanked; therefore I am. . . .

My mother spanked me, hit me, struck me . . . she did it because it worked. It brought her quiet, acquiescence—it was *incredibly effective.* And now I'm trying to avoid, at all costs, that efficacy.

I want to keep him from my mother-me. So that he won't become me.

* * *

I am increasing. Becoming publicly pregnant. Pregnant so you can tell. I like laying my hand on my belly, a beatific Mary. The truth is I am laying my hand on pushed-up stomach and intestines, not the tiny fetus that sits squarely above my pubic bone. *Now my belly is as noble as my heart.*

Where my skin gave way before, a shining. When pregnant with my son, I couldn't see them, so I didn't know they were there. Then the mirror told me, after he was born. *Stretch marks*—there should be a better name for them. My midwife Tawnya's belly is striped like a tiger's.

The results of the test come back. Negative. We are pleased and repulsed.

My mother calls to ask me for my address because she wants to send me some mail addressed to me that's come to her. *What street do you live on? What's your mother-in-law's name? The husband? Where do you work?*

The baby is well. My mother, not so much. So what shall we do with her?

I'm angry about her memory, angry with her for getting old.

* * *

While my son plays, I try to divine his future face from the one he wears now. My mother says I look just as I did as a baby, but of course this is only true for her. When I see my son, I realize how easy it will be to infantilize him when he's thirty, having known him so needy and small. I see now in his face the careful concentration he will show a lover. He stacks blocks somberly, as if I am not there.

I see my young brother in my adult brother's face. He is the first child I knew other than myself. My brother's eyes still contain the naiveté I liked to abuse. My son has my brother's eyes.

My son wakes up and says, *Wait a minute. Ice cream truck.*

That my mother is mother to two others feels like a contradiction. When do I think of how my brother or sister might feel mothered? Never, she's mine.

My brother and my sister making a place for her in their lives, what that place is like. Since they both live near her, they get to see her more often.

All three of us so different. How did we come from the same place? My brother is my mother's precious son, an impulse she inherits from her heritage and culture. Apron strings and a blind eye and desperation toward his peccadilloes.

My sister is her baby, unexpected, later in her life, after my brother and I were both in school. She found out she was pregnant during an Army physical. She was trying to remake our life with the military, had a baby instead.

And the one who fancies herself most like her mother is the one farthest away. Through a series of strange stumblings and coincidences I ended up in New Mexico, this flat, dry desert. Venomous insects live around the edges of my house. Today I killed a centipede in my son's room. It was living inside his garbage truck.

*   *   *

Now my husband and I agree on a boy's name, in the event we have another boy. We like that it's a literary allusion, but, even more, that no one will notice the allusion. He will be a boy who has a little trouble in school, who is less gregarious than his older brother. One summer he'll make a birdhouse with his uncle and become smitten with carpentry. He'll go to college and discover a knack for architecture. *My father wanted to be an architect*, he'll tell his advisor in college. He will become an excellent draftsman. He will have a tattoo of a house on his upper arm.

*   *   *

We plan the second birth like veterans.

When I decided to have my son at home, my mother asked my sister, my brother, my cousin, my aunt, anyone to call me and tell me that I'm crazy. She wouldn't say it herself, because she knew what I might do with her disapproval. For her, it's two narratives with the same plot: one in which she loses her mother from birth and one in which her daughter reenacts that scene.

Birthing at home had nothing to do with her disapproval. If it did, I didn't and don't know. At the time, I thought we decided because hospitals smell bad and because that's where people go to die.

We decide to have the second baby at home, too. I wonder if it will alarm my son to hear me in pain. When he hears any despair or sadness in my voice, he cries. I slammed my finger in the door and screamed in pain, in terror. Why? Because his mother might die? His food? His succor? His *Chi-Chis*? I hope I go into labor right after I drop him off at the babysitter's, deliver the baby right before picking him up.

We first decide to have my father-in-law take my son to his house while I birth at ours, then to have someone with him at ours while I give birth. I imagine listening to the strains of *Sesame Street* while a huge contraction overtakes me. I imagine how the moaning bloodiness of labor will translate when he's in therapy.

When I gave birth to my son, I had one day of irregular and mild contractions. I watched *The Office* boxed set while stretched out on the futon next to my brother-in-law, then one night of standing in the bathroom, plotting my escape to a hospital for a cesarean. A chopper to carry me away from this hocus-pocus midwifery to nurses and epidurals.

We had a birthing tub set up in the living room for my son. It seemed to be going so well in the water. I felt capable. I moaned heavy from my chest like the women in the video. My husband sat on the inside and played deejay: The Orb, The Future Sound of London, music for birthing in space. I got out of the water and things fell apart. The scene caught up with me when I pushed for two hours with nothing to show for it.

I had to stop pushing because I wasn't progressing. The midwives told me to walk around the backyard, swivel my hips like a belly-dancer. I was furious at the seeming frivolity of the request, the touchy-feely-ness of it. My husband held me up as we walked around our pitiful backyard, dug to pieces by the dogs, only sand and small patches of grass, greener than green had ever seemed.

Until that moment I hadn't known my husband as I thought I should. *The person you choose is someone you would feel alright with in life-and-death levels of tripping.*

I fell so deeply in love with his calm in this.

The desire to be driven away from the pain passed. In our backyard I felt a resolve I didn't recognize as part of me. This was it. My reckoning, my mettle time, my boy was coming.

Born on the futon in the living room. I was stunned by the chaos, the disorganization. Fluids and sweat and endorphins. *These were pains one could follow with one's mind.* What I said when he was born: *That came out of me.*

He shivered on my belly, my hands shivered on his.

Placenta, from the Latin: flat cake. At our childbirth class while watching a video of a birth, I was impressed by my comfort with the gory screaming—until the placenta emerged. I gagged. So when my placenta emerged, I asked not to see it. Kamy and my husband studied my placenta, talked about how old it looked. It's an organ you make and then give up.

*   *   *

My son's word for *Sesame Street* is *adeet.* Sometimes he watches two in a row and I shower, check e-mail, fold laundry, load the dishwasher, clean the bathroom countertop, stained toothpaste gray. He sits mesmerized by Rosita and Elmo, by the flashy performance of 7, the number of the day.

I never claimed to be a mother that wouldn't let her kids watch TV. If I did, I didn't know what the hell I was talking about. It feels good not to *be* the TV.

When I question myself I always invoke Abraham Lincoln's mother in that log cabin. Except there's a TV and Abe's in front of it so she can churn the butter in peace.

My husband gently suggests that our son is watching too much television. He might as well have suggested that I am drinking in the morning or bringing home hitchhikers. I fume for hours and then spend the rest of the day constructing an argument I can barely sputter out that night.

We jealously stand guard over our personal time because we're both writers working too much. We both want the same things—but only one of us is a mother.

I wish tedium upon my husband, long stretches of domestic anhedonia. I wish him hours of laundry, of dust, of conquering strange smells in the baby's room.

I think: Better a child well versed in *Gilligan's Island* than a mother in a padded room. Better a pop-culture blogger than a mother who irons his underwear because somewhere along the line *she lost herself.*

My husband takes it back.

From an old notebook of mine: *They were lovely, the tulips. Went to the Schiele show. I sat on a deck chair in front of a fountain and wrote for a while.* I can hardly bear it.

My personal time comes at a larger price. I want to find a number value for it, but I don't have the time. It seems like two and a half to my husband's one.

Both writers, but I've made a compact with this life, the old promise coming back to haunt me. Not just our old promise, but the promise of motherhood itself.

The work I do to make our presence in the house invisible is invisible.

I can't admit I need the writing like he does. Or he doesn't believe me: *Wolf, wolf.*

I read depressing books about resolving husband and wife conflicts. People conduct studies about children ruining marriage. *Yes, I know! Amen, Sister!* I imagine running away to become a waitress at a truck stop, my son tracking me down after years of searching. He peers into my haggard eyes, says nothing. Leaves a photograph of his family with his tip. His stepmother's a blonde.

Then I think: foolish, foolish. I love my husband too much to bean count.

And the other one, the one inside me, unformed and unknown, still a mystery to fall in love with. The first time around, I was infatuated with the process of it. Now what?

Now I take comfort in the familiarity of pregnancy. The old shoe of it. Every little twinge once sent me running to the books. Now I self-diagnose, I cure.

I grow into my mother, I grow old with her.

To settle into how it isn't what we dreamt with our Barbies and their suitcases, plastic babies with curled-up legs.

At my age my mother had three children, three jobs, a failing marriage. Yet in pictures she looks pretty, never defeated. As a child I looked at her photos all the time to try and get at what she once was. A smile always broad and dazzling. Her shift dresses, the wigs she wore to make her hair seem straight and beehived.

In college I wrote poems about these photographs because I thought I was supposed to write about beauty and mystery.

I am obsessed with how my children will look back at images of me. I think to Photoshop in some joy, some thinness.

My mother has only two or three photos of her own mother, having had to share them with four sisters and her father. What my mother learned about mothering is preserved in amber. Her mother doted on her those nine years she knew her.

The mother in my mother's heart.

Because they aren't many, they are the same stories about my mother's mother: everyone loved her, liked to confide their desires and worries to her. Her children were all that mattered.

Like you, I tell my mother.

No, she insists. *My mother was a saint.*

*   *   *

A long day at home, no work. Full of resentment.

I want to be in the world today, in my past when I could walk out of the house without looking back. I want to go the store without the struggle of the *car seat.*

My thoughts turn to violence. To rage, screaming. My father's mother would say, *Me das rabia.* I thought, Rabies? Rage thus became scary, foamy: *She would bring down the little birds.*

I remember, at the age of four or so, antagonizing my mother. She snapped and dragged me to the bathroom, put me in a cold shower. I shrieked as the water struck my clothes. She closed the curtain, returned a few moments later to turn the water off. Wrapped me in a towel, deep into her arms.

Is this abuse? I wouldn't do it to my son, the cold shower, the volatility of it. But I understand the impulse. I yell. I rage. I imagine terrible scenarios I would repeat to no one.

Pillows, knives. *Mütter,* murder. The word *suffocation* has mother buried in it.

The books say to count. The books say count to ten, but ten isn't enough. I count and count and count. I count aloud and he counts along with his own numbers: *J, X, X, J, A.*

When counting doesn't work, I count the soft-spoken moms in the park standing in the room with us—*judging*.

They're the mothers who remember the snacks, the ones who use cloth diapers. They are efficient and demure. I don't go anymore because they're so good at it.

My mother's rages passed on to me, into me.

*   *   *

He's taking it all in. He's starting to remember. No chance to start over now. It's the beginning of his real life, also the imagined one that he uses to explain the real one.

Mama, talk about my friends.

The imaginary presence in his life called Duwaduwa curls underneath for cuddles. My son gets amorous with Duwaduwa.

My son's got a temper like mine. Duwaduwa soothes him, but Duwaduwa is ephemeral. Days will pass and we will hear nothing of him/her. Then I'll find my son with his face pressed to the floor in his room. He stares vacantly and I know that he's got Duwaduwa with him. It's a world I don't know. I worry about it. I relish it.

When he is a joy, I think: foolish, foolish. He is puckishly sweet when he hugs the dog, when he lays his head on mommy, when he kisses my lips with his teeth.

He talks in his sleep. So few words. Already they spill over.

When he started talking, I wrote a list of his words in a notebook for two months, then stopped: there were too many. Some words were mysteries. He repeated and repeated them. I was taken aback for not knowing my son's words. *Yesh* was not yes: it was something to do with the television. *Mama, dada, noway, bowl, ball, bird, box. Book, bug, more, dude, door, duck, juice, eyes. Hi, bye, bubbles, happy, whoa.*

Acks was both key and light.

The look on his face the first time he sees a train in motion.

On a bus, he engages a woman's attention. He tells her about himself. He points to me and says *mama*. He points to my belly and says *baby.*

He listens to the words I say and makes approximations. That he speaks English because I do. That I should teach him Spanish, my mother tongue.

My lexicon and his as the same thing.

*   *   *

I google womb. I google Alzheimer's. I google prepartum depression.

I see a midwife and not an obstetrician because I don't want to treat pregnancy like a disease, but it's certainly shaped like one: symptoms, signs, sickness . . . the way it alerts and alters my sense of the body.

My mother calls me to review my symptoms. I return the favor. We counsel each other to take better care of ourselves. We share some symptoms: my brain is stewing in estrogen, hers is losing dopamine. We're both forgetting where our keys are.

Her doctor suggests that she take antidepressants for her memory, but she's convinced she'll get addicted. She says she'd rather forget things.

My mother asks me if I've been to the obstetrician, and I again remind her that I'm seeing a midwife. It's not her memory, though, in this case: she really can't believe I'm not seeing an obstetrician.

She tells me that someone recommends she take *uña de gato* for her hands.

My mother doesn't understand why our midwife puts off our first ultrasound until after the twentieth week; she thinks they should scan me at the first possible opportunity to determine the baby's gender—because she wants to start shopping.

And when do you see the obstetrician again? she asks a few days later. *Soon,* I tell her. *Very soon.*

*   *   *

My son and I curl into each other. His feet are perched on my legs like he's on a springboard. I touch his ginger hair, tell him a story about a glass-bottomed boat. Green fish, blue fish, polka-dotted fish . . . until his eyes close.

My son sleeping beside me. And then the one inside of me finally moves.

I clean my house ravenously. The beds are stripped and aired. I insist my husband paint the hallway, the bathroom, sand and paint the children's bookcase.

At night I stay up late scrubbing at the grout lines, at the food-encrusted highchair. Because of this, because I am the housework wraith, the one who stays up all night building the cobbler's shoes to save his life, my days suffer and suffer.

Because you'd like control of your life, says my imaginary therapist.

I fixate on the edges of things: the baseboards, the windowsills, the corners of my house. I spend a day picking dog hair off the rug in the living room while my son begs me to do a puzzle with him. *No thank you,* I tell him. Then: *No thanks.* Then: *No.* Then: *Leave me alone.*

We hire a housekeeper to serve as a mediator between the house and me. I want to leave her a letter that explains why I needed her to come and clean my house. We leave in the morning and when we come back there is nothing left for me to do. Even the bathmat is spotless.

Because I begin again and again. Because I am supposed to be enjoying my child. Because it means so much these days, a little wiped-off spot.

I am ashamed of my ordinary desires because they are not wild artistic desires or sexual feast desires. I want a magic wand, but only to clear the laundry basket of its eternal load, to spirit the bacon grease off the counter.

We hire a housekeeper even though we can't keep up with the credit cards. I don't know how else to do all of it. How could I?

Why should I?

Should is a fraught word in motherhood. Motherhood is full of shoulds. I should get back, I should pay more attention, I should iron that.

I should. To should or not to should?

We pay her discreetly, praise the work, lead her to the door. I speak to her in Spanish because it's easier—and because it reminds me of home. She's younger than my mother, although her work and her life have made her older.

Her name, Socorro, means *help*.

After we're sure she's gone, we walk from room to room, marvel at how clean the house is—like a hotel. We order a pizza so as not to muss the kitchen. That night there's a thunderstorm, which scares the dog, who pisses on the bed. All of it together—the housekeeper, the thunder, the dog piss—it all resonates like a good haiku.

The housekeeper becomes a shame, a pride, and a vantage point.

My life of piss and shit. The Martyr mother with worn-down fingers. The *Imitation of Life* mother.

Because, I remind myself, this is what I always wanted. A family and its headaches.

*   *   *

I begin to resent my son's breast-feeding. My husband tells me that at night, while half-asleep, I yell at my son. No memory of that.

My husband performs a *weaning intervention*. He sits me down and explains how my crankiness is affecting our lives. He has a plan. I'll sleep in one room, he'll sleep in another room with our son. He'll help my son to sleep.

I weep. *He needs it,* I say.

He needs it: I need it.

When my son was born, my midwives told me to give breast-feeding six weeks. My breasts felt like they'd been gnawed on by rats, but I persevered because I didn't want a kid with *allergies,* with a *smaller brain.* Then the six weeks passed, and my breasts healed. Nursing calmed me. The books said: Oxytocin.

To not have his head pressed to my body like that is why I wept and wept.

I try to begin weaning him by emphasizing that he is a *big boy.* But of course he isn't. He can't even open a door. But I want myself back so bad. I tell him, *Chi-Chis all gone.* He assents, asks, *Chi-Chi all?* My heart is broken. But I don't want to be a hero; I don't want to nurse two babies. I hear women talk about doing this. They're the same women I hear talking about sewing their own clothes and potty training their infants.

To wean: to unaccustom. Doesn't quite describe how it gets when I deny him the *Chi-Chis.*

He pulls at my shirt crying *Chi-Chi!* He scoops his hand into my bra. I distract him with chocolate. I'm weak, don't know how to do things the hard way. Let him cry, says one of the books.

The breast is a machine that produces milk, and the mouth a machine coupled to it.

When I nurse him, I feel like I am filling him with myself. What I can't say out loud, what I can't manage to give him in the day, I give him through my body.

We postpone the final-total-weaning day. We promise him a party, on the advice of a therapist.

He holds his head against my chest nearly all day. We are castaways. He cries weakly for *Chi-Chis*, but now he's becoming resigned. Is this his first disappointment?

On the night reserved for one last nursing, he nurses fiercely. I feel duped. He bites and won't let go. I scream. My husband wakes, but not my son. Sated, he sighs and turns sideways. My husband and I both slide to the edges of our bed.

*   *   *

All my life I assumed my mother breast-fed me. I discovered she hadn't when she watched my midwife teaching me to breast-feed my son. My mother said, *I wish someone had taught me when you were born. I wish I had been able to do that. It was a different time.*

Duped again. Sure, she had given herself over entirely, but who knows what her dreams were, really? But I wanted it to have been more, all. To have been nursed and solved that way.

From her notebook: *Shoes and a matching purse. Dyed? A gold watch. Lord and Taylor chocolates. A record player. Invisible ink.*

He wants me to stack blocks with him on the floor. The one inside me presses against my lungs. I can't breathe. I'm no mystery, I am source. He's perplexed when I don't simply respond to his every demand. *When did I get so complicated?* his expression asks. *When did saying yes get so mired in me?*

His expression says: *There is no you here anymore.*

My mother, a mystery this way too. No her there.

Every night I tell my son the story in which he goes on an adventure with a girl he likes, *Lena*. The castle is filled with magical rooms in which he searches for a giant fish. He sleeps with his face against mine. He strokes my ear.

This is a new stage of our love affair. I can't understand how I might love anyone else as much. How it was when he was born and how my love for him was at the exception of everything. Motherhood as the state of exception.

Some mornings, my son stretches out his legs onto my body. I hate feet, the look of them, their job, their dark lives, but I love my son's feet. I rememorize them every day. The nails are chipped in places because I don't trim them. I love their sweaty smells that tell me he's doing some living. His feet are soft and supple, like moccasins. We call them mountain feet.

My son plays a game with me in which he pretends he is leaving for work. He asks, *Mama you sad?* I pretend to be sad and he and I hug and kiss good-bye. He rides his little scooter out of the room, chuckling. I pretend to cry. He runs back in the room and says, *I'm back!*

When I leave for work, depending on my urgency, he'll wave me off, ask me to please leave now, or hang on my legs like I'm never coming back. Often I'll simply slink away like a thief.

Is he leaving me behind or hearing me long for him? Fort/Da.

*   *   *

At night, my humors are all wrong. Bile rises in my throat from drinking water. So I stop drinking water. My lips dry. My son and husband snore as I dig in the cabinet for Pepto, as I trudge back to bed to ensconce myself in the barricade of pillows that prop me up, only to do it again three or four hours later.

At night, my hours are mine. When afflicted with heartburn, I sit and stare at the ocotillo outside our window.

Our giant bedroom: only a bed and a dresser. I make plans to paint, to put up blinds.

I plan while they sleep. Our future lives, how to protect them from grief and disappointment. And when that gets sorted out, I conduct imaginary inter-views with Oprah. She asks, *How did you manage to have it all?* I lean back in my chair and explain. That part I can't hear.

I creep back into the bed and he sleepily mumbles, *Cuddle.* He wants to press his face into mine and play with my earlobe. Warren Beatty seduced women at parties by placing his hands upon their faces and holding their faces to his. When my son holds my face to his, yes, I am seduced.

Motherhood as a passionate love affair.

*   *   *

At a park, a woman I don't know tells me my son should be wearing a jacket. Two things happen. My head says *Go to hell,* and my mouth apologizes. I'm sandwiched between who I was and who I must be.

*   *   *

The body and its symptoms. Bleeding gums, constipation, moodiness, cramped fingers, stretch marks, swollen tongue, forearm rash. The body hazing me into motherhood. Sciatic pain, restless leg syndrome. The body and its sadism, hip spasm, brittle hair. The body in rebellion.

The body deformed, the silhouette exaggerated.

My mother's symptoms. The same question over and over. Lost keys, forgotten appointments. The twist of arthritis in her fingers. Some kind of pressure in her head, she says.

My mother gets an ultrasound of her head. A small dark blur in there.

Her doctor says the tumor should come out within the year. She calls to tell me that it's the kind of tumor that grows in the breasts, begs me to check.

It's in its own sac, the thing in her head.

We wish together, my sister and I, for the brain to absorb it like a fetus absorbs the homunculus. We also try to imagine what it's like in there. When I was very small, I imagined a crib inside my mother's body. I lived in there, a little red bedroom.

She says there's too much to remember. Her doctor tells her to keep a notebook and write down all the things she needs to remember. Now she has a real notebook.

Finance company, compañía de teléfono, llama Jorgito, la Macy's.

I buy her a nice notebook and put it in the mail to her. She never gets it.

I tell her to write down how she feels, what she thinks. She asks me why.

*　　*　　*

A woman's story begins with her parents. The kitchen can tell the house, Mami said, and the mother can tell the child. My children tell the story of what I made my life, more than a mother, more than its half, and then the part where I give over to my own mother, strong center: once in her body, red bedroom, all the way until the year nineteen forty-six. Youngest of four sisters: Esperanza, Elva, Olga, me.

The years between her and my children. Those are mine.

Mami always wanted to be a mother. She was good, mothered Flaca's kids plus kids who begged in the streets, left some food on the patio of our little house. I remember the smell, the coarseness of her hair. Part of my own body. I grew beneath the shadow of a tall, strong woman.

Jealous of everything, our neighbors, my sisters, she emptied Papapa's pockets for what another woman may have left behind. We handled her jealousy, fragile object, never using it to hurt her, though we could have. One day might have. I know what it feels like, then with my older sisters, now my own daughters.

She sewed us dresses envied by all. She said, All you girls behave. Today I am going to try and get money from Papapa so I can make you more beautiful dresses. You must show him that you are good.

A country, she was my matria. She knew only the life she had, the sisters she had grown with, the Lima and Iquique she remembered. It neither bothered nor saddened her. It's the way it is.

I could tell you her face, every pore. While my sisters played outside, I lived under her skirt like a cat. The pudding, the songs. Mami died before we could hate each other. Could this be a gift?

No: A woman's story begins when she separates from her mother. But then mine would begin with an ending, end with the beginning, the shortest and longest story I know. Mami, one moment everything, the next, nothing. Now me, my children. My mother behind me, before me. Now grandchildren. A series of relations that tells me and connections that root me to the world.

I can't tell it, the story whose beginning and ending have switched places, so it stays inside and burns. The word I can't repeat, the word-wound, because of its size. A train passing through me, the flashing windows, I see her on the platform for less than a second. Sometimes she never existed and I came from nothing. But for a word she said, maybe a sentence: her death replaces my birth, they are the same thing. . . .

I make her body a holy place in my mind. Maybe to love the Virgin Mary. Bare canvas upon which to paint our backwards story.

From an old notebook, top left corner, a child's handwriting: 14 May 1956. Today my mother died. This is something I will need to remember.

A doctor on TV says that a baby girl is born with all the eggs she'll ever have. Me with my mother all her life and my children all my life with me. A woman's story begins. I tell stories for the ghost of a girl inside me, a mother on the outside. The doll with the matching outfit.

Today I left everything behind for a day and went to the ocean. I threw my apron in the water.

*　　*　　*

I am in one bedroom, my husband and son in another. Screaming and crying drifting in through the air registers, it's only an abstraction of grief. In spite of myself, after wallowing in the profundity of his pain for an hour or longer, I fall asleep.

Next morning, we congregate in the kitchen like roommates. My husband is weary and discouraged and I pretend not to notice. I slept better last night than I have in months, years, decades.

The second night, I take to my new room like I'm at a fancy hotel.

Next morning, despondent, I return to our bed and sleep while the two of them curl into each other, far on the other side of the bed.

*　　*　　*

Two hours before the first ultrasound. Loudspeaker announcement of baby's gender impending. My mother phoning all morning to remind me I would be going. *This* she remembers.

Fetus, infant, baby, blastula: the context and occasion.

Like my husband, I want a daughter. I once thought it was narcissism that compels people to have children. I feel embarrassed for wanting an image of me, flattered that he does too.

The years in which a daughter and mother are at war, each other's mirror. A sister to my son, advising him about girls. A daughter to my husband, who asks her to choose earrings for me. *A flourishing, hidden tree.*

Or two sons hiding dirty magazines in a fort they built with their dad. Two brothers reminding each other to call me on my birthday.

In the darkened room, the technician squirts cool gel onto my belly. My son keeps yelling *bitch*, which I translate to the technician as *beach*. My husband and I both know he is really saying *bitch*. I regularly yell the word when I drive.

Hopefully, the worst thing my kids will ever say about me was that I had a dirty mouth.

In the darkened room my son alternates between sitting on my legs and being held by his father. He doesn't like being kept from the drama on the exam table. Bluish shadows appear on the screen as the technician rubs the wand across my belly. I tell myself I see a face, maybe a leg, but the truth is I don't know what I'm seeing until she tells me. Then the shadows coalesce, suddenly, the truth of a person. There is the baby's face. Its hands are by the face.

Spine, kidney, liver. All made from my body. *These are her girl parts,* the technician says.

Her body gave her away.

When I call to tell my mother, she can barely stand it. She asks me what I will call the baby. I tell her. Moments later, she asks the same question and again I tell her. *Ruffles and lace,* she says. *Patent-leather shoes. A girl like you.*

Boarded the train there's no getting off.

Daughter, I whisper to myself. *Daughter.*

I will infuriate her. She'll resist the sweaters I pick for her. Often she won't take my calls. She'll date bland boys of whom I disapprove, wild girls of whom I disapprove. She'll make an effigy of my disapproval and she'll marry it. She'll be me and I'll hate it.

I will laugh with her at the lady with the dog next door. I will talk to her three times a day about nothing. She will send me pictures of boyfriends, of girlfriends. She will ask me eagerly, *What do you think?* She will send me poems she's written.

What I might leave her if given time, I might write on the front pages of all my books: *For My Daughter.* And maybe one day she might write in all my books: *Once My Mother's.*

I grow into my mother with my daughter. I grow old for them.

*   *   *

Pregnancy: a state, the delicate condition, bun in the oven, in a family way, knocked up, eating for two, eight months gone no end in sight. Waiting for the stork. Bone tired. Creaking. She lies inside me like I'm the beach, all stretched out and nowhere else to go. Something has got to give. Nothing available.

Each time I talk to my mother I get sterner. *Are you getting enough sleep? What medications are you on? When is your next appointment? Is this doctor any good?*

She asks me the same exact questions.

My mother blunts my worry to save me from it. It's an old wives' way: Keep worry from the baby so she's not deformed by it. Carry low and you'll have a boy; carry high, a girl. Don't you dare eat strawberries. Heartburn tells the hair.

Monday's child is fair of face;
Tuesday's child is full of grace.

We keep ourselves away from each other. We are fearful.

My daughter changes the character of my pregnancy. Now I say *her* when I feel movement. And I mourn the story of two brothers, just a little.

Grandparents pleased all the way around. I'm proud.

*   *   *

Words don't come easily to my son. He stammers, looks in the air, wags his finger as if pointing me to what he really means. The struggle hurts my heart—this loss for words—because so much of what he wants to say has to do with needing.

We want to tell each other the story of what's happening to our selves.

Mama, did you dream about my penis?

*   *   *

Are you my mommy? Mama's boy. *Heather Has Two Mommies.*

My Mother the Car, baby mama. Mommy Wars, MILF, Hipmama,
MomsUnite. Mother-of-pearl. Motherboard, Mother-in-law. Mothers Against
Drunk Driving. Mother Earth. Yo mama so fat. *Mommie Dearest,* mother
lode. Mother may I? Mothership Connection. Sierra Madre. Sometimes I feel
like a motherless child. The refrigerator mother. The good-enough mother.
Mother Russia. My mother done told me. *All women take after their mothers,
and that is their tragedy. No men do, and that is theirs.* Soccer mom. Alma
mater. Mother hen. Mother Superior. Red-hot mama. Earth Mother and Holy
Mother of God.

Paradise is under the feet of mothers.

*   *   *

My husband is unwilling to provide a guess as to when I'll go into labor—but it's all I do—guess. I want to receive an appointment card in the mail with a kitten hanging from a tree branch, a bubble of dialogue above the kitten's head, *"Hangin' In There."* On the other side: *You will be giving birth on April 1, 2006, at 4:55 p.m. Please call to reschedule at least 24 hours before your scheduled appointment.*

Home stretch, last lap. Third trimester. Her due date falls smack dab in the center of the semester. Someone phones in a bomb threat to the university and class gets cancelled. Thank you, bomb threatener. Thank you, dear bomb threatener. Thank you, bomb threatener, for the extra day with my feet up.

These days I feel I'm *owed something.* Which is the culture that showers sweets and adulation on pregnant women? I ask my husband to google it because I've performed a self-abnegatory google intervention on myself.

I write little notes here and there. In a few weeks I'll be typing with one finger, a baby with dream-twitching eyes cradled in the crook of my arm.

There is little room for me in my body. My daughter unquieted, I enjoy lying on my back because the books say not to and because it stirs her up.

And the thing in my mother's head, made in her like I was. Cells after duplicated, interloping cells.

She'll be fine, I repeat, I repeat, I repeat. Mantra.

Protecting my daughter from my mother's illness, pushing it away from us both.

My mother's body could hardly keep me. Our bodies were incompatible, hers attacked mine with antibodies. I was delivered, yellow and livid, unto a world of transfusions and tubes.

She says she prayed so hard her eyes hurt for many days.

*　　*　　*

For two weeks, prodromal labor. *Precursory, or preemptive*, Kamy says, although that possibility fades on day three. *Prodromal*, sometimes called *false*, cruelly. One night I shuffle, shuddering and shivering up and down my hallway wrapped in robe and blanket. Nothing like I thought it would be, this labor, like it was promised by all the well-wishers: second one always easier.

Prodromal labor is the first lesson my daughter teaches me. What we will do together for the rest of our lives, either decipher or encode each other's problems with time.

My mother recedes, although I talk to her every day. *Now that I know*, she tells me, *I feel better.* I dart in and out of her world, that's all I can handle. I call my brother and sister and ask them to act as my ailing-mother emissaries.

And now here's my son growing charming. *Mama, joke,* when something funny happens. *Mama, ache-ache?* when I'm writhing in bed. When he was born, I made a pact with myself that he would never once see me cry. Pact now suspended. He soothes me, using words I use to soothe him: *Sokay, mama. Sokay.*

Mama, hold you. Mama, cuddle. Mama, work? Mama, fix it. Mama, clean it.

He talks to his sister through my skin. He wants her to come now so that they can play now.

Nights, I hear him from the inside of my pain, affording everything a hollow, tinny sound. Our routine is constructed around my pain. Tons of takeout. I slip into my bathrobe and wrap myself in the blanket, failed metonymy for: *This is now beginning.*

Pain as message. Pain as practice. Pain as matter. Every prodromal night I tell myself that I am *bigger than the pain.* Generous with it, surrendering to it. Platitudes about pain I read in books. I am, all of a sudden, the scholar of pain.

Pacing the hallway because the laboring women from the prenatal class videos pace. Useless pacing. The dog loves it, though, trotting alongside.

One day the pain becomes more painful than pain. *Go to the hospital,* Kamy says.

A nurse straps me to a machine that measures my contractions. I'm in prelabor: because of this pain-beyond-pain. My other midwife, Tawnya, arrives. She talks about her drive over while she takes my pulse, then explains away the terrifying wavering lines on the printout from the machine. The choice I've made: a hospital's rude machine and my tattooed midwife counting my contractions in her head while telling me about her new belly-dancing class.

They tell me to rest and give me pills. They tell me to come back if the new superpain comes back. My husband and Tawnya hustle me out of the hospital like we're leaving a shitty party. To tell my mother, to not tell her. I want to shield her from my anxiety: there were a few minutes there when I thought I might lose this baby.

But I need her. I need a mother right now.

We make light of it on the telephone—it's what we do with trouble. I tell her about the uncomfortable bed, the cold room. She tells me stories about being in the hospital, hearing a storm of diarrhea in the bed next to hers when in labor with me.

We stamp down crying and offer our happy voices instead. The O. Henry story in which the couple sells their treasures to buy each other a gift meant to embellish their treasures. She calls again and again and again. Her anxiety becomes a charm to prevent anything bad from happening.

And then one night, no pain; the next, a quick and violent storm, the pain comes and the pain's gone. I am back to being *just pregnant.* The kitchen calendar: eleven more days minimum. This one plans to stay as long as she can.

She tells me as much, in the terrifying adolescent voice I have created for her. Same voice she uses to tell me she's pregnant, same that she hates me. It's the voice in which she one day says to me, *I wish I was never born.*

Languid malaise, but I don't call it that because of the *mal,* the bad.

Pregnancy and superstition: I'll believe in whatever if you promise to get this thing out of me.

My husband indulges both my naps and my insistence that he change our son's every diaper.

These are the days in which I want to teach my students like I love my son. I want to play with their hair. I want to tell them stories with castles because it's all I can muster.

How children influence and alter our work.

How I have two lexicons. One of them waits patiently in the parking lot in his car seat.

*   *   *

On the day before she is born, I chair a graduate student's thesis committee, my belly shaped like a bullet. We talk about arrangement, estrangement, derangement.

My colleague and friend Connie, pregnant too. We two are four in the room.

I'm hoping I'm talking like I'm not pregnant? The non-mother, I'm hoping, professor with the slender belly.

Night. Prodromal or real? I crawl about the floor. Call the midwives, tell my husband. He says, *We have plenty of time.*

My body is pure transition. *All our progress is an unfolding.*

I sit on the toilet, but imagine myself sleeping in bed. This girl doesn't know her body. Becoming mother: as estrangement.

I crawl about the floor while my husband is in bed. My histrionics shame me. I want to be the birthing mother who has an orgasm. He learned the first time around how to measure a woman's cervix. *Please,* I say. *Check me.*

Cockwife, I call him.

It's different, he says, his fingers in my body. Near this examination my son sleeps quietly. The light in the room diffuses the moment. The dog's collar clicks against the floor where I rest my head. I listen for the coming train. Becoming mother: as derangement.

I am on Death Row. Where's my last meal, my tranquilizer? Dead Mother Walking. I assess what's around me, shape of room, light of bathroom, my son's repose in our bed.

My mind wanders, altered by fear and boredom and pain. How must my mother's head feel? That I spend time thinking about her tumor in terms of fetal development, a living, changing thing. Will it be born tonight too?

My husband calls, the midwives come. In the interim, I fold laundry on the floor in anticipation of guests, pause for contractions. Becoming mother: as arrangement.

I am disappointed for these reasons: No birthing pool, and where's my Boards of Canada CD? I am thrilled for these: My son sleeps, and it's almost over.

Call your dad, I say to my husband, so as to not have the bother of worry over my son, the thing I most fear.

Five minutes after the midwives arrive, a moment after they've put a chuck pad under me, I feel a pop in my stomach. I think she's exploded.

Dead. What would that have meant? *Do I still have to push this dead baby out?*

They tell me the pop was my water breaking. Then the thrum of her heart-beat. Like gulps of water.

The endless pulse of the pregnant body. The circular time of my body, my mother's, my daughter's.

I say, *Put on the Brad Mehldau*, any music that might reach inside me and calm these bothered nerves. A laserlike curing hum. As a child, I suffered terrible stomachaches, and my mother would rub my belly and hum rhythmically. Where's that CD?

I want her here, but not her terror. I'll shield her from my pain. From seeing any suffering, even this kind. Becoming mother: as estrangement.

I won't be pregnant anymore, and that is where the emptiness begins.

My mother hovers over my labor even though she's a thousand miles away. Time pushes me rudely through the works of pain.

Afraid to push because of last time, when I was bullied by my body. *Do I have to push?* I ask. Tawnya has become my friend, so I feel less need to appear proficient at this. She has witnessed my ineptitude at other things.

I summon the eighth-grade race in which I ran the mile. The pain, but how I managed—ashamed to stop.

No, your body knows what to do, she answers. She rubs my feet. All the erotic energy in the room from my body: the reaching, sweating, pulling, the smells. I'm at an orgy.

Time, its tethers loosened from me. And mine from time's.

My husband squats behind me, literally holds up my body. Also figuratively.

Between contractions like between takes in a film: we joke around, relax our shoulders. Kamy's lying in the hallway with the stomach flu, unable to move.

No, I won't push. Because of last time. Passive descent. My body forcing her out. My mind doing nothing.

Descent. Decent, distant moving away. I try to fly from the moment in my mind.

I push, I know the shapeliness of her body. I push again, she crowns then sneaks back in. *One step forward, two steps back.*

I push. She emerges. Crying. Ugly—pugilist ugly. No one was ready. I am proud. Proud I was efficient. Proud to be proficient.

A story from my mother: When I was born, the nurse wheeled me into the room from the nursery in one of those clear bins. I was wrapped in a pink blanket, and my mother was still disappointed about not being able to name me Natasha; she would let my father choose a name. Then it occurred to her: This pink bundle. I have to take home. For good.

In the body, a baby is saved from its mother's terrors of pragmatism. Conceptual baby.

When she tells that story, it is about terror, although she doesn't say so, and that is why we laugh. *How can it be about terror?* she laughs ironically.

She and I have been bound by terror these past months.

Being born has battered my daughter. There's an inverted triangle on her forehead where she passed through the birth canal. Her nose is tilted to the right. Already thinking of her beauty because I know she might need it.

She's covered in blood, vernix, mucus. Her first coat.

Her mewing is nothing like her brother's, shock number one.

My body is wasted and spent, barely here, and yet still I take her, desire already flowing.

I want to hold my son one last time instead. But he is sleeping with my father-in-law in the other room. I didn't know that this birth would be over so soon. He doesn't yet know how this house has changed.

Someone helps me up; I wobble like a fawn. Who has the baby? The house buzzes in my ears. Someone puts a blanket over my shoulder. It's my Sesame Street blanket from childhood.

In the shower, afterpains, bleeding. The thud of adrenalin in my heart. To stand here a while longer to hide from my daughter.

A hollow in me now that she isn't there. A felt absence, intense, fluid desire, I don't even dry off before she's in my arms, trembling. My love has fractured. I love two children.

When I hold her.

When she's against my body, eating me alive, alivening.

Fits me like a key. She's my book.

*   *   *

Our family means something new in this bed. We are four.

A child is a blessing. *Blessing* once meant *consecration in blood.* A baby crowned in her mother's blood. This mother blessed twice.

My uterus shrinking inside my body. Old, wet shoe contracting in the sun.

My son gets whisked away by a series of relatives and friends. He's with us long enough to hit the baby. His body looks strange and clumsy, so big next to his sister's tininess. Hysterically, I ask myself, *Do I still love him?*

Connie brings champagne, chicken, bread, cheese, pesto. We eat like it's the only food we've ever seen. She holds the baby, rests it upon her own huge belly.

The phone, the phone, the phone, the phone, the phone.

I ask for my mother. Don't know when she flies in. Don't worry. She's coming. I need her, how I need her. How to explain it?

When my mother finally arrives, I show her the baby as if it's something I've made exclusively for her. She holds her awkwardly, afraid. She's forgotten about babies.

I look her over closely, examining for the tumor's influence.

She kisses my daughter and me, leaving us the scent of her perfume and the mark of her mouth on our cheeks, which we wear all day.

My son takes my mother into his room and closes the door. Loud laughter. She's bought him coloring books, sweaters. She's bought my daughter enough clothes to last the next six months.

Moving all about the house, she's looking for ways to rescue me. *What can I do?* over and over. I make a list of tasks for her, the ones that seem herculean to me: putting contact paper on the shelves in the kitchen, running the vacuum cleaner throughout the house. Soon the coffeemaker gleams. She does what I cannot, what I will not. She performs these tasks because she doesn't know what to say.

*   *   *

My mother and I lie in my bed with my daughter asleep between us. She tells me the story about the conceptual baby. Because she's told it to me before, I have been protected from that terror. I want to explore some other terrors with her, but I'm too ashamed. One question is simple. *Are you going to die because I'm at the cusp of things and all other questions I might ask are actually that same question?*

We gossip instead. *Gossip*, from Middle English: godparent, spiritual adviser, female friend invited to a christening.

We begin with celebrities, but the conversation quickly turns to our family and their lives. We critique, dissect, examine. *She wears the pants in that family. She doesn't have a good relationship with her sister. She doesn't always want her children. How does she find the time? And her husband . . . and her children. . . . How she keeps her house, so messy.* Then we theorize, that's always the best: theoretical gossip.

She asks the same questions over and over. *And where does your friend live now? And did she get married? Kids?* Because of her head and because of the thrill of this new girl.

She should look at herself in the mirror before she leaves the house. We're cruel tourists in other people's lives. *Her husband's putting horns on her.*

I study her face to find the illness. See if she's changed. My fears so small in her light.

Afraid my children won't love me when they're grown on account of my flaws. Afraid that I can already count the mistakes. Afraid how failure could be disastrous in this case, not like all the other ones, those commonplace failures amounting to the half sum of my life.

We fall in and out of sleep in the giant bed. Adrenalin renders my dreams chaotic. I dream from a thread of my waking dream. That my mother comes to be with us always. That we pass our caring around like a ring. In the dream there's way more than there should be.

She'll be a dancer, she says. *A scientist,* I say.

She cooks for us the only thing she knows how to make. *Lomo saltado.* A plate of childhood.

She doesn't cook; I don't cook. I am my mother's daughter.

To me she is two things: (1) Oz behind the curtain. (2) The curtain.

She was once the center of everything. I remember wishing for a different mother because I felt the draw of her too strongly. Now she's the Special Guest Mother. We stay up late watching TV. I regret it, am relieved by it. I don't tell her when my sister calls. I want to spend all her mothering before she goes, wring her dry of all the mother in there.

*　　*　　*

When I come to my son's bed, he holds onto my neck. *Don't go mama.*
Longing has entered his heart, and his brain is complicated by it.

Not less, just differently. He's shifted from the center of my world to its half.
I orbit two suns.

His ideas about the world, I collect them to press them into the book of our
history. *Mama, thunder isn't afraid of the bubbles.*

*Mama, why were you screaming when the people took the baby out of your
body?*

*　　*　　*

We look on the Internet for her type of tumor. I read and reread the numbers aloud to her. I tell her what her surgery will be like from what little I've
gleaned from these Web sites. Most of what I tell her comes from having
watched so many TV hospital dramas over the past twenty years.

She accepts my information like it's scripture. Since I was a child I've aided
in her passage through the world of the United States. She's better than most.
She has a job, speaks English well. But she defers to me because I've mastered
English in a way that she didn't. I talk to doctors and make plans. I parent
both my mother and children through language.

I imagine what the surgery will truly be like: a doctor standing over her
draped head, the crack of her skull, exposed brain. I do it to strip it of its terrible power over me.

We make plans beyond her surgery. I will take her to Paris someday. We'll
buy fabric in the streets to make curtains for my house.

When is my flight? Twenty minutes later: *When is my flight?* Twenty minutes
later: *When is my flight?*

I want her to stay with me and take care of me because *that's the way it's supposed to be.* I am about to return to work. My thoughts bend away from the warmth she's made of my home. On the day she leaves, she weeps. *I don't want to go* . . . like a daughter I'm marrying away.

From my mother's notebook: *And then I went away for good, and I left it all behind because ahead of me lies an adventure requiring no one but me.*

*　　*　　*

When I first came to this country—a lark, a gang of friends entranced by New York—I worked in a cafeteria, Savarin, in the basement of a giant insurance company building on 59th and 6th. I couldn't speak much English, and the patrons knew what they wanted, ordered without the small talk of some restaurants, numbers on the menu. I knew what no meant and I knew what yes meant. Once, someone said, Not yet. No yes? What is no yes? The other waitresses in the restaurant coddled me, most of them immigrants from Europe. They remembered what it was like for them. My husband worked in the restaurant upstairs, first as a busboy, later a prep cook. We were together all day.

On days off we went to Central Park to watch the hippies dance on their spread-out blankets, the tiny transistor radios they brought. The music shivered me. We made enough money to pay our rent, to buy records and food, and we could still buy hot dogs and ice cream from the vendors on the street. I did not know then that I should be afraid of walking on the streets at night.

Today the phone rings—one of my children with questions about the surgery. My daughter wants me to sell my house and move in with her so she can watch over me. That cannot happen.

Some people believe you know the moment of conception, you can feel the first moment of pregnancy. I was too busy becoming a wife. Marriage made love formal. I wanted to be a mother so badly, if only because I loved my husband. That's how I understood motherhood then, family-making. I found out because I missed my period. The doctor said, Yes, you are pregnant. Time to take care of yourself.

Time?

Of course I was happy. I could hardly stand it. I didn't know what it was. This is me now, looking back at that girl and realizing that she was 22 years old and had no idea what it was about, no perception of the scope of motherhood. I went to stores to admire baby clothes I could not afford. I ate voraciously. The distraction of the city. Silver burnish of the quarter, the gleaming abundance of apples at the grocery. Tall, handsome men. I was Alice in Wonderland fallen into the world of Sofia Loren and Raquel Welch. Those were the bodies that mattered. Still, I felt lovely. A tightness in my uniform, soon I would look like a mother. My uniform was a miniskirt covered in yellow flowers. I looked like one of the hippies.

I thought, This is it. Yes, it felt like the end of something. Now I know that the beginning of one story marks the end of so many others. No Europe, no becoming an actress, and I wouldn't sing backup for Neil Sedaka. I had, without thinking, given myself over to this life. Nothing to be done. Despite the inevitability, or because of it, I was thrilled all the same.

Some days I worked the cash register at Savarin. One morning, as the workers with newspapers tucked under their arms came from the subway station to buy their coffee and Danishes, I felt my gut rising in me, rebelling against my work. Sharp and dull, the hair on my arms standing on end. Thinking on it now, like men becoming werewolves in movies. Monstrous. Between customers, I knelt down behind the register and threw up in a bus tub.

I worked with a woman called Fiji. She was from Germany, and she told me that the throwing up was part of it. She fed me crackers like I was a small child. Even now, forty years later, I remember Fiji's gold and pearl earrings pulling down on those meaty lobes of hers.

One night we went to a party at Fernando's in Brooklyn. Since I was the first one pregnant of us all, the gang treated me like a princess. Everyone scrambling around getting me things to drink, pillows on which to rest my swollen feet. Fernando lived in a basement apartment and, although it was spring, it was hot and dank. I danced a little, but mostly I sat and watched as the others danced. Mancini, Herb Alpert, Sergio Mendes. All I could do was imagine the child inside of me. A boy, I knew. I could see his face, saw in it his desire. I spoke to him inside of me. I hoped he would be tall like his father: narrow shoulders and green eyes.

The pain came early in the morning, waking alerted by an ache in my stomach. Pain like disaster, so improbable . . . the child inside had seemed so permanent by then. I was a sinking ship, nothing to be done.

Now they have science to explain what it is to lose a baby. My daughter tells me from her books what she thinks might have gone wrong. But that moment felt like my failure, not my body's. No book for the most enormous grief. I thought I'd live inside it forever. I taste it in my mouth, even today.

In the bathroom, my son draining out of me, into the toilet. I thought of taking the bits out, to the doctor, pleading for the salvage of my son. The reason for which a parent lives is to shield her child from such pain: the loss to make ridges on the heart.

Of course now I have my three. If I hadn't lost that baby I wouldn't have had the daughter I have now. To look at her today . . . every consequence colludes to create this.

When pregnant again, I made so many bargains with the world. Took better care of myself, whatever that meant at the time. Although I still had to work hard, Fiji carried all my plates out. She forced me to sit with my feet up every two hours. I worked until my eighth month. The regulars brought clothes for the baby.

The other waitresses held a shower for me. Piles of gifts. I didn't know what most of the things were. A young girl, no idea what it meant to become a mother but that my body was telling me that I would be one soon. It could have been dangerous for my children, how little I knew, but when she was born, although there was some fear, I was brave. I had been efficient, now I was proficient. I was proud.

*   *   *

I am the mother. Like that. My outside life calls to me. This might be the reason maternity leave exists, to undo yourself a bit from the outside world. A cushion between the start of it and the acclimation, but I'm worried about the student who comes to class very occasionally but is brilliant, and the student who struggles with depression, the perfectionist.

No one can do it like me, I reason.

After a week, I start making noise about going back to work. No one protests: a surprise. I want someone to stop me from this folly. I call my mother, who insists I quit my job if they take me back so soon.

On my first day back, I try and find clothes for my deflated body. I'm ashamed to wear the maternity stuff, but that's all I have.

I walk into the classroom like the new girl. One person fewer than myself. My students are quiet, shy, awkward—because of how much my body is in the room.

I want to tell them about what having a baby was like. The pain in my womb, angry red scribbles in the margins of their poems. Instead I am cursory and distracted. I give them group work and let them out early.

*   *   *

Work, home, work, home. Like a timer, my breasts leak at work. I end class early, rush home to my baby, who needs my body, who my body needs. Work, home, work, home, work, home.

Homework?

I stand on the brink of an abyss of wonder. I am crazy with hormones and this impossible schedule.

Six of one. Half a dozen of another.

Now while I teach, my family sits in the parking lot just outside the building, both children strapped into their seats. We bring them so that I can feed my daughter at a moment's notice. My cell phone feels like it belongs not in my pocket but in my bra. It seemed foolhardy to have our bodies so far apart. I rush out of class, pulling at my clothes, Wonder Woman changing personas. Work, home, my daughter crying for hours.

I feed her in the parking lot or under a tree or on the curb.

Sometimes she's in class with me. I'm in the back of the room feeding her, trying to keep my body from my students.

There's no you here.

The students file in and out of my office with their excuses. Dead grandfathers, crashing computers. *Bah,* I say to all of them—except the mothers. Before my own motherhood, I excused the mothers with stories of ear infection or chicken pox in honor of my own mother's hectic schedule. Now I commiserate with them silently, sometimes aloud. The impossible life of being a mother along with anything else.

I tear away at my clothes, running through that parking lot with the first flush of a love affair. Pushing down the door with my body.

And she cries and cries. She cries so much she becomes emptied out of crying, a wide-mouthed, red-faced muteness that I can't do anything with. I worry that she's crying because I'm a working mom and she disapproves.

Between crying jags she sleeps, the angel in the pictures.

When not sleeping she's ill-tempered, boorish.

I can barely stand my daughter at night. Is it the blues or something more? Lack of sleep? I never suffered it before. I fancied myself a Ben Franklin, full of invention.

Colic? Fussiness? Temperament, inheritance, will? Hurry up and become two, like my son, and play contentedly with your guys on the windowsill.

In the dream, I am in a Lifetime Television movie, shaking my baby. In the next scene I am taken away in handcuffs. To sleep.

Work, home. Lottery Fantasy. Work, home.

One day, while my husband is away, a boy comes to the door. He is almost a man. He says, *I have a school project. Is this a bad time?* I move to block the way into my house. Neighbors are so far away. Who is this boy to come and disturb my peace, scare me for my children? I hold the baby, close the door to a crack. *Yes,* I say. *Bad time.*

*   *   *

I take her to our doctor because she is yellowish red. She suggests blood tests. I will see my daughter's blood. So soon.

I'm ashamed to ask about the crying. *Well, what did you do to her?*

Well, what the hell did you expect?

The doctor calls to say her bilirubin levels are high. I imagine the brine of bilirubin stewing her brain, making her deaf, just like the Internet says it will.

I examine her diapers to divine her humors. Yellow bile. Choleric. Colic, suffering of the colon. I rub her rigid belly, massage it, force out the air. I hear everything that happens in her body, a tiny ecosystem, mirror of mine. I listen for an answer in both our bodies.

I tell other people about it, hoping to come upon the Colic Witch, who will give me the spell to end all this.

The difference between night and day becomes indistinguishable. She stiffens her body and cries fussily at 8 p.m., keeps it up until 11 p.m. or later. I watch medical shows on mute with captions. We sleep in the spare room because her crying and my despair keep the others up.

I work so hard for our peace. My books are collecting dust on the shelves. I pace the room, rocking her, humming, turning on the radio for white noise. We walk around some more. I feel like an actor in a commercial about motherhood, but no violins.

My friends Sheila and Connie teach my classes, grade my papers, piece together the working person I'm supposed to be and do it for me.

My mother calls and asks, *How are my girls? My kids?* I want to tell her about despair, but she has her own brand of it. Growing old and tired. I wouldn't want her life. I tell myself that I won't have it.

Or her head.

I'm sleeping well. She's such a good baby. The kids get along fine. Don't talk about unpublished poems collecting cobwebs. About the houseplants slowly dying on my watch. About my irregular grading practices while breast-feeding.

Would she have complained? and to whom? I don't want her to have the ache of my dissatisfaction. So then I think, *My daughter will publish if I don't,* insomniac logic. All the things I have ever wanted from life, she will do.

My daughter as a dancer, as a singer. Little Carmen. I'll force her into a tutu, into a room with Keats and Sylvia Plath, a notebook and pencils.

Sorry to leave you with such incomplete ambitions, my notebook will say to her.

*　　*　　*

In a sleepless haze, my ghost ministers to the children, their needs, and their protestations as I watch from the couch. Becoming part of this so as to not become a part of this. They don't notice. The ghost coos at them and tells them I love them.

Thursday, where did it go? It seems like only yesterday it was Wednesday.

Always hours away from sleeping. An island I'm swimming to that looks close but is many miles away. She squirms in my arms, makes soft crying noises.

She has more in her. I think to tell her about my life. I pretend she is the interviewer listening with rapt attention.

I tell her once there was just me, it was all me all day. I tell her the details of these days.

C—— once had a trim, unfettered landscape of a waist. She let boys, for whom she didn't care, fall madly in love with her.

Carmen lived in San Francisco, danced on the patio of a gay bar called the End Up until noon. Carmen smoked clove cigarettes. Carmen went clothes shopping, spending half her paycheck every other week. Carmen wore high-heeled boots. Carmen dated a younger guy her friends called Jailbait. Carmen wrote poems in front of a window overlooking a broken-down gazebo.

C—— didn't know about this part: that no one would rescue her.

I can only imagine our lives together one day at a time, because if I try for more, I start crying. I count her age in hours. Mute the TV and read the captions, note what is badly condensed or what is omitted. I predict endings aloud and I am right nearly all the time.

When Surgical Tools Are Left Behind 2. The Mermaid Girl. The Man Whose Arms Exploded.

Sex and violence, cosmetic surgery. I watch movies in the middle, Brat Pack movies because they remind me of high school. Molly Ringwald before she had babies. Watch them while I read. Hardly hearing the TV because of the baby crying or my son singing about rubber duckies, mute and read the captions while I read a book.

I watch shows about actors and their disastrous lives. How I wish for their disastrous lives.

Because of time and impatience, I just read the endings of the movies on the Internet. I am a big-time movie actor in my mind, my children being watched over by nannies.

Do their big houses smell of urine?

Their big houses descended upon by gifts and nannies. Scented candles and organic Pine-Sol. Their children as tiny cashmere-wrapped parcels. Air kisses.

I call my mother, even though both kids are crying. I have all but closed the door in my children's faces, the little one too little to be left inside her crying. She says, *Me parte el corazón cuando lloran así.*

Partir means *to split.* Her heart is split. *Midwife* in Spanish is *partera.* Heart-splitter, the body splits in two.

I call to hear her tell me something, anything about a life outside of mine. Her gossip: my lullaby.

My daughter might cry forever, that this is her temperament. She is *that* girl, the one that cries at the tip of a hat. The one that will pierce her tongue and listen to This Mortal Coil in her headphones.

Ghostmother of shrill sunlight. Saint of eye bags. Queen of wafting attention. Cursed daughter.

Then one night, I put her down on our bed for a moment, for a break. I check my e-mail, read the news. When I go to her for our nightly thing, she's already asleep.

I say nothing, try to think nothing for fear she'll hear my thoughts. Knock on wood. Throw salt over my shoulder. I pray to everyone I can think of.

Same thing next night. Infants and the discrete blocks of time of which their lives consist. Little boxes of disorder chained together.

I report the progress to my husband, who has been sleeping in the other room with my son. We once scoffed when we heard people did this. *Sleep apart? We're married, for crying out loud!*

I can look at her again. Her gestures replace memories of my son. I pore over photos of him to make sure I'm not misremembering his childhood, confusing his with hers. They are one thing packed together in my *tightly wound devotion.*

At the same time, I fret over how she's different. She arches her back when I try and hold her for too long.

Her voice is thinner.

The yellow is finally gone. Nails are pink. She holds her neck up a bit. She's getting prettier. I imagined this moment when I was pregnant, wished for it. She's forced the days to gallop past us.

The way she falls asleep next to me, the way she stretches out her little body, and the grimace her mouth makes when she stretches. I finally understand what *button nose* really means. How her mouth reminds me of mine. Changed.

One night I become a bit accustomed to this life. Then the next a bit more, then the next.

The Ziploc in the freezer I've mistaken all these months for a cold pack is actually my placenta, between the peas and the Eggos.

*   *   *

At my age my mother wore the polyester blouses and the platform shoes of her day. She mothered and played lovely at the same time. Shaved her legs, wore rollers in her hair. While I load the kids in the car, I assess my mien. I never wanted to be the hipster mom with the nose ring, the belly poking out from under a tight T-shirt. But I had never thought about what the alternative might be.

Does my fat ass make my fat ass look fat?

My mother in a tight polyester blouse, a miniskirt. Wearing a wig and false eyelashes. I'm holding the edge of her.

What story does my mother tell about me? What story will I tell about my daughter? *Etc.*

One day after work I nurse the baby and watch a TV dating show in which young men take girls' mothers out on dates and choose the girls based on their mothers. *Date My Mom.* Mothers who make coy jokes. Mothers who flirt like they're on real dates. Mothers who behave stiffly like chaperones. My husband loves my mother. He is patient with her, would choose me through her.

Does he really choose me? Because I am a mother and changed by it, I feel I need to be chosen again.

When was the last time someone photographed me? My face is the one taking pictures, my eyes creased for each one of my children.

My husband watches me mother, and I try to impress him. I want him to want me for this.

*   *   *

The days divided into two: working and mothering. The third part, which is me, lives in my dreams.

Dozens and dozens of decisions to make each day. Compromises, negotiations, inventions. Motherhood, the invention of invention.

How do I hold two children when one wants to be read a book—*Mama hold it*—and the other wants to nurse? How do I handle simultaneous screaming fits? Which one do I choose? When my husband is sick or at work? These questions are monolithic.

In college I waited tables, which required me to think of many things at once. I had nightmares about wandering away into the woods after taking a table's order. Now my nightmares are about falling asleep and waking up not knowing where my children are. Suddenly it's dusk deepening outside and I barely know my name.

A speculation: my mother did not manage this by thinking of herself.

And now my daughter knows my face. I can never leave and I can never die.

I examine a day like it's a tree, rings telling me how many layers away I am from sleep. I read an article in which a woman fell asleep and her daughter drowned in a bucket of water. That kind of tired.

Tired, tired, a tyranny of tiredness. There's *time* hidden in *tired*.

Tired becomes ether that refracts time. When I am in it and there is no end in sight.

Tired. Bone-tired. I think of escape. To get out of one's cape.

So . . . fucking . . . tired.

I wish I was Swedish or that I lived in some suffragist's conception of the twenty-first century, with nurseries on the floor of every building.

Still, I wanted this. Small hands, pads of fat on top. As a small girl, I held my three-year-old cousin's hand and said, *Yes, someday this for me.* Is this why things change so slowly for mothers? Because we want it?

We're afraid to say something because it might get taken away? *I'm a cloud congealed around a central object.*

What did I think mothering was then? And when I found out I was pregnant? How did I think I'd become a mother then?

*　　*　　*

I find little bits of time to myself. My daughter sleeps in her Moses basket, and my son busies himself with his fire truck.

Their faces in the backs of my eyes, reflected onto my laptop. In and out of the little spaces of my days.

When I resisted writing about them, I had nothing to say. Now I spend entire days composing around them, around me through them. Motherhood is my subject and my object.

This is the secret world of the oracle. How can you hope to understand her before you know what she is really like?

I can use them to tell my story. They're the explanations for this section of my life: Part Two.

I'll leave them clues in my poems. My biggest thrill: that they'll care and read what I write to know me. That they'll say, *I knew that about her.*

*   *   *

I bring my daughter to class on the last day of school. As if to say, *This is what happened to me.* My students take turns holding her while I teach.

I feel that same joy I felt as a girl on the last day of school. The throwing-notebooks-in-the-air feeling. Lassitude-anticipation feeling. I should have given birth today.

To figure it out so no one is affected. Not my students, my boss, not my son, my husband. Not even myself. A fantasy.

And my mother living in the back of my head, fretting endlessly over her health. *What does it feel like?* I ask her. *Like there's always something there,* she replies, *over me and in me.*

My children are the scrim through which I see her. My students thank me, shake my daughter's tiny hand, say good-bye.

*   *   *

We'll remember this as my daughter's first summer. Point of reference for future summers. We go to the university's swimming pool, the pool I love because of all the public mothering.

I'll remember the way my husband left her in the sun too long, her face made lovely and pink, also my first scare for her life. How she lolled in the car seat covered by towels, the cooing that strangers did over her. Their faces. I'll remember putting on a bathing suit and missing the expanse she made of my belly. My son, less afraid of the water than the last time.

This is my son's third summer. He digs his fingers into my hand when kids in the swimming pool get rowdy. He hesitates around the edge. My son has golden hair. It curls, it traps light. I look like the nanny with my mother's olive skin, black hair. In my lap, he's my prize.

It's personality. He is tentative around slides, rides, and boisterous children. He has his own brand of wildness. He doesn't like to be bothered by other children's conceptions of play. He's acting out the stories in his head, complete with voices. Anthropomorphizer of napkins.

In the pool my body floats, and I allow in all the ideas I miss about myself. A flossy rope ties me to myself. A leash. Heavenly mother. In the swimming pool I am a child making angels in the snow.

Other mothers swim in the pool with their children, many of the mothers older. The sun adds a glisten on the ends of their hair. Their bodies underwater look unearthly. The woman in the lane next to me has shoulders as wide as my grandmother's.

We wrap our children in towels the same way: so that their bodies are swallowed warm with them. We hector them about sunscreen.

When I swim and I am entirely alone with my thoughts, my children pass through my mind only as *topics*.

I think, *Today when my daughter and son lay together on the bed sleeping. His lanky body next to her curve. Is that not a poem?*

Her come from your body, Mama.

I try to remember the writing ideas that escaped me the night before. The ones I was certain I would remember. I couldn't get up and write because I was wedged between my children's bodies. Now I don't understand the lines.

Divided into lanes, the pool is cleaved by the ghostly bodies of mothers gliding back and forth, back and forth. We are all submerged away from our lives. A woman's daughter stands at one end, yells, *Mom, Mom, Mom,* and we all look.

The water's tender cradle—it lifts my body back into place. I hear sounds like my daughter must have made just two months ago.

The mothers at the pool slick with water, they appear emergent.

Tired of thinking of poems, I plan her college years, her wedding. I invent her a big loft apartment in New York.

I'm swimming for blankness, but it doesn't come.

Out of the pool, immediately back into it. My daughter pushes her head into my wet body. *I want to hold myself to you but you are myself.* She's hungry and it's late in the day.

She is lovely with her heartbreaking. She takes no notice of me, what I think of me. Just my body.

As I swim and lift my head to breathe, I catch a glimpse of the world they're in and then recede back to my temporary world.

Motherhood as pastoral.

Motherhood as transcendence, laden with immanence.

Motherhood as tenancy.

My husband walks the length of the pool as I swim it to meet me at each end. My daughter's big imploring eyes. I ask him to stop.

I sit and talk to a beautiful woman about mothering. I tell her of looking at my daughter's face for beauty, something I didn't do with my son. I remind myself to look for strength, for intelligence in my daughter's face. The beautiful woman asks why.

The beautiful woman speaks of being occupied by the thought of pregnancy and asks if it's strange to have something so big in you, so living. I am reminded of how gradual the occupation was and thinking this was biology's way of adapting a mother's body to its eventual split.

The beautiful woman has never been pregnant, wants children. I tell her she would be a good mother.

We can all of us only try to be good mothers, I tell her.

I felt occupied, I tell her, when my daughter's presence gave me heartburn. When I couldn't sleep. I couldn't explain how it felt like my body had been finished. That would have been sentimental.

It'll change everything, I say instead. *But in a good way.* I hope she has children. I hope it goes like it went for me.

Every girl here the future age of my daughter. Every boy the lean body of my son. I hate to live so much in the future, but it obsesses me. That they will discover literature, that they will have political leanings. That their bodies might have scars on them. A series of futures. I will them past my end. Rattle my bones like they're charms.

Back in the water for one last swim. My mother can't swim; I feel proud when I tell her I've gone swimming. She's afraid of the water, its depth. She's afraid of my going far down into the water, going away.

I tell her about the swimming back and forth, and her fear breaks the day into pieces. She's making a day and night of it.

When I was a child, I was terrified of the water but swam anyway. My cousin lived in an apartment building, and we'd swim in the pool at night, the lights casting our twisted shadows against the walls. I never closed my eyes.

One night, the lights blinked out: a short, a timer. Who knows? I called out, *Mami, Mami,* like she might save me. She came to the edge of the pool, kicked off her shoes. She would have drowned. She would have saved me and drowned trying. Just for my fear of the dark water, its lascivious lapping against the wall.

I go swimming for her and against her. I go swimming to take her into the deep water in my heart. I swim as her.

*   *   *

For a couple of weeks we pretend that my son has a *bedtime*. We put him in his bed and close the door. I nurse my daughter, put her in her crib. Then we climb into bed like they do in the movies. We turn on the little lamps on our nightstands, set books in our laps. I listen to my iPod, and my children sleep peacefully. My husband and I entwine.

I am impressed with how tidy I've made my life. I begin to enumerate other mothers I know who haven't got it so tidy. I wonder, *What's wrong with them?*

More books appear on the nightstand. I buy magazines, make lists, take notes for a book I want to write, plan remodeling projects. Then the baby gets an ear infection. Then my son has a nightmare, and now we're back to the disorder we really are. Once again, a word spelled in four letters on my bed at night.

It's the small collapse of order we made. Happens every day. *Happens to all of us*, my doctor comforts me. Perfectly normal.

*   *   *

Because it's Father's Day, the weekend of the U.S. Open, my husband travels to see his father in Kansas with our son, a thousand miles away. I pack a huge bag with my son's world in it.

When they drive off, it occurs to me to run after them, stop them from making a big mistake. How could they leave me alone with a baby? How could they go away from me? Alone, then it hits me, and I let them go.

I am left alone with my daughter. I imagine being left alone with my son, then remember I am bound to my daughter in a way that is past with my son.

I don't dare tell my mother about their trip until the last possible moment. I don't want her to imagine me alone, afraid of the froth she'll get in. Her fears infect and paralyze me. Her fears are so far in me, I sleep with the cell phone on the bed, one push of a button away from 911.

Her fears displace mine. A fear contest. An anxiety tournament.

My daughter's gaze is a trap. The infant's flat mien. The absence of speech. Infants are secrets.

When she sleeps, I feel alone, and this makes me glad. She sleeps besides me in a world of which I am the absolute center.

My daughter's head near mine: smells of sour milk, electricity, still a faint smell from inside my body.

I used to count a new love affair in weeks. When the weeks became months, the love affair began to feel substantial. I grew to know some stranger. Today my daughter and I have passed three months together, and so our familiarity means something. I'll buy her flowers or write her a funny note.

I compose songs with her name in them. I whisper her name like I once whispered boys' names to my pillow. Boys that broke my heart. A name to make the heart ache.

Lullaby: to hush to sleep, to say good-bye. The lullaby with cracking branches.

*   *   *

What to do? Half my life is gone. Like a robot I career off the walls, overloaded with What To Do. Stupidly, I use one of her naps to organize the cans in the cupboards. Her next nap gets delegated to *America's Next Top Model.*

I make long-distance phone calls to long-lost friends. Who I am spreads through the house like the smell of gas.

What To Do finally turns into sitting in fits of time, into writing bits of bits.

*　　*　　*

Connie gives birth to her daughter, and I want so much to tell her everything I know. My new sagacity.

To remind myself? As consolation?

I am jealous of her tiny baby, my baby is ungainly in her advanced age. I want a fresh baby.

Sheila and I coo over her daughter, then over her. We'll be three mothers together, drowned by love.

Her anxieties rustle up the ones I remember. She's pacing the room because her daughter won't eat. That despair. The first night of my son's life, he cried and I could do nothing for him. How that realization made the night eternal.

Because of how lonely it was. Love cloaked in despair. Urgent and hungry.

I want to solve Connie's problems because I wish someone had been able to solve mine, but they're complicated, like folding maps.

To see her mothering excites me; it's another part of her. There's a natural part to motherhood and a quickly acquired one. *There are no amateurs in the world of children.*

Sheila and I have a list of things about mothering we pack into a little basket that she can use: how to go about not letting it exhaust you or eat you alive.

We tell her what we know to be true. *A woman is always hampered.*

It's not twice as much work, it's more. At least you know what you're getting yourself into. Get plenty of rest. Don't worry about the top of the refrigerator.

Fussed over by women all my life, I crave that ministering tonight for Connie. I'd like her mother to brush her lips on her forehead or touch her finger to a crumb on her lip. I wish to be tiny again and in my own mother's body, to make her young and become nearly invisible doing it.

* * *

The narcissism of motherhood. I need her because she made me. Because she loves me for my daughter.

In a photograph, her wide face, the curly hair that frames it, is like my mother's. My mother in her mother's arms.

My daughter smiles when we wake up next to one another. She sleeps while I clean the house and wakes up when I finish. My breasts ache, signaling the end of mopping. She rolls over now, one arm stuck underneath her body.

When they return from their trip, my son is a little older, a little more himself. He is somber when he kisses me hello.

I tell my husband to tell me everything. 1,001 nights of my son. I want to know each new word, observation. Did he cry for me?

I study his face for some information. I ask him, even though I don't have a fully formed question. *Sorry 'bout it, Mama.*

He comes back with a train trauma that makes me furious with my husband. I want to take my son back into me and wash him of it.

The train trauma is daunting, like the fear-of-falling-off-the-changing-table trauma and the dust-bunny trauma. He's going to be made of these things. I knew a woman with salt trauma, a man with balloon trauma. They set you on a certain course.

The Mother That Worries Him Into a Corner. The one that worries him into a worry all his own.

When the train whistles, we remind him that it's so far away.

My son says, *Don't worry, Mama. Trains come and they go.*

* * *

My mother tells me about her finances like it's her secret life. She asks me to write her a will in which I divide her belongings between my sister, my brother, and me. A bit of her house and her bank account for each one of us. She worries about the government taking her money.

She's worried about leaving something behind.

She's telling stories now, not keeping them straight. They're about not being tired, about not being afraid. Someone's going to remove a part of her, and she asks me to write her last papers.

Las Cruces is a place where people go to retire, so we often go to garage sales and estate sales to kill Saturday morning. We finger the stuff of old ladies, the stationery they thought they might use, antimacassars stained with coffee, the clip-on earrings their daughters passed over. I cannot force myself to imagine going to my mother's house after she's gone and sorting through her things. These things either become useless or priceless in her absence.

Motherhood as balm for old wounds.

Mother, thicker than blood.

When my grandmother died, there was so little left that it was easy to divide. We still find pieces of her life in my mother's garage. The thing I wish I had, something stolen in the hospital: her tiny jade Buddha.

Another way my mother is a mystery: the way she cared for her mother-in-law, even after my parents divorced.

My mother-in-law's other car is a broom.

Because her own mother had died when she was so young, was what I thought.

She tended to my grandmother—who was childish, volatile, jealous—with such tenderness. We joked that she was my mother's older daughter. Because to lose that . . .

There should be a word that only signifies a mother's death—a word fricative and loud. Especially now, because we are waiting for the words that will not be enough.

My daughter has my grandmother's eyes. I am sure she will be a little bit her.

My daughter has her thumbnail as well, which I let grow in order to see my grandmother's thumb. I will paint it when she is older.

My grandmother tended to my mother's feet with a little scalpel. She scraped the corns from my mother's toes, rubbed them with lotion. A job only a mother could love.

My grandmother collected pictures of the Virgin Mary. Christmas cards, devotionals, ads from magazines, pictures cut from books. She put them all in a photo album she would take down for me. For each viewing, I decided which Mary was my favorite. On one day it would be Raphael's *Madonna del Granduca*; another, a soupy Cubist watercolor from a '70s Christmas card.

I was choosing the mother of us all. Penitent eyes cast heavenward. *Hail Mary, full of grace, the Lord is with thee.*

Where is that book today, my grandmother's book of mothers?

From my mother's imaginary notebook: *Remember their faces, the foods they loved, and all the places they've ever hidden.*

My mother loved her like a mother.

All her life my grandmother wore bright red lipstick and Coty translucent powder on her cheeks. She made me paint her fingernails twice a week so that she'd never have a chip.

She smoked cigarettes outside, afraid that my mother would find out. A daughter. If she was angry with my mother, she smoked inside.

She dyed her hair black and styled it like she had for fifty years, Elizabeth

Taylor in *National Velvet*. She answered the phone, *Yes?* She ate saltines with butter and tepid tea every day at noon.

She loved sweets, hoarded them in her room.

My mother knew her longer than she knew her own mother, just as she's been in this country longer than in her own. She was with her when she had her first and second strokes. She put her in the nursing home, stayed at her side as she died.

Almost all daughter.

*   *   *

The glow of my lamp next to my bed, the pink of my daughter's pajamas suffuses her face with vitality, with health. Her blue eyes. How much longer will I have to dodge death to see her through?

I'd like to marshal her every cell into normalcy.

But I can't, won't. It's out of our hands. *En las manos de Dios*, my mother would say. In God's hands—but I can't. It's not enough.

*   *   *

On the last day of summer I tap the keyboard gently at night while the house sleeps. I will not let the tyranny of light sleep rob me of my little snatch of time.

Snatch of time, a stealing away, robbed of time. I am running out of it or away from it, but it's always catching up. *The only currency for which I care is time.*

Sometimes I catch myself off guard, spring upon myself the question: Art or motherhood? I know what the answer is supposed to be, but sometimes I say the other, just for the daydream of it.

My logic becomes childish because that's the part that wants it at all costs.

The Bohemian Mother. The Daffy Mother. The Mother with a Studio in the Garage.

From a book about motherhood: *Motherhood in our present social state is the sign and seal, the means and methods of a woman's bondage; it forges chains of her own flesh and blood; it weaves chords of her own love and instinct.* I'm embarrassed to be crying.

The well-groomed house as a work of art. The five-course meal as sublimated art. The well-behaved child as *objet d'art.*

It is terrible to hate one's own heart. My joints ache at the thought of it.

Renunciation of repose, of leisure. Renunciation of appetites. *True liberty is not defined by a relationship between desire and its satisfaction, but by a relationship between thought and action.* Renunciation of doing.

I don't want the dignity that motherhood offers. I often reach the point at which my parents would have flipped their lids. The point at which, when I once witnessed it in other parents and children, caused me to wonder why those parents weren't yelling pinching pulling. And yet somehow I'm not pinching pulling yelling.

I'm working so hard to undo what got done.

But one day my son slaps me across the face. A straight-up *bitch slap*. And within a microsecond of his hand touching my face, I slap him back. *Stronger than all my afterthoughts is my fury.* Wow. I'm *that* mother, the one yanking her kid by the arm out of the grocery store, the one who gets really close in her kid's face and hisses.

The apple doesn't fall far from the tree. The Spanking Mother. The Mother Trapped in a Cycle. I tabulate the long-term effects as I weep in the bathroom, as my husband sits on the other side of the door. He is furious and forgiving. Me too. *Mama, hold you.*

To return to her . . . to repossess and be repossessed by her. Don't know where my anger comes from or where to put it. To retreat into myself: the dream I have. To undo whatever moved me to hit him. I am a history of mothering.

It goes so fast, it all goes so fast.

I call her from work, and she tells me she feels pressure in her head. The whole thing loosens her from our prescribed roles: she's telling me things like she's afraid and sad. She doesn't want to bother me with this for long. She tells me that every day she kisses my children's photographs. Talks to them with the hope of seeing them soon.

I tell her about the slap, placing her between her loves.

She comforts me. Mothers always do, even the killers.

Trying to think of my mother's head overfull. So what's getting pushed out?

Her mind as script, as calendar. . . . Her mind as artifact.

I want to tell her a story because that's what mothering is all about.

*   *   *

My sister calls to talk about our mother's failing memory. It's a conversation that makes us feel as if we're big and little girls alike. We pretend to make the huge decisions, as if she might let us mother her. We conspire against her because we're so afraid. We bully my mother with our worry because we're desperate for her to be well.

Then I call my mother to hear her strong voice, because I feel guilty that I think she's helpless. Prattle about the weather, the kids. I laugh and hear her in it. She tells me she's getting the surgery soon . . . but she's like the daughter who lies about where she's going and where she's been.

Where to put her, old mother. *Into the yolk and white of the one shell.*

I call my daughter *Mamita;* my mother calls me the same. Little mother. Layers of mothers.

*   *   *

I hand my children over to one of the babysitters I've brought into my life. I hear the babysitter's voice through my door saying what I should be saying.

My mother asks who helps me with the kids, and I can't answer truthfully because it will never be enough. Did she want another thing too? She says no, but these days I don't believe her. I believe you have to want another thing.

She had her things, details about her that I remember, like her singing in the car despite our protests. Watching *West Side Story* and weeping at the end like this isn't the twentieth time she's seen it. Dancing at the parties we'd go to as children. I'd fall asleep watching her *cumbia*. Her dreams: to own a business, to own a Cadillac, to go to Italy.

Or her other thing, which was always us.

*   *   *

She calls to tell me she would like to take us to Disneyland. It's worth a million dollars to her, she says.

When I was young, we lived in Anaheim and we'd go to Disneyland back when they sold tickets for each ride. She liked to take us because of the spectacle. If someone were to look at my childhood photos, it might seem like all we did was go to Disneyland. She took me there for the first time when I was 18 months old. My mother and my aunt dressed my cousin and me in matching outfits.

She took us out of school to take us for our birthdays, even when we couldn't afford it.

She asks, and because all her desires are fraught with mortality, we agree to go, and she calls us every day until the trip. She remembers how many days are left.

She asks me if I need any clothes for the trip. I know what she wants. *Dame el gusto*, she's taught me all my life. It's so easy to say yes.

We all do, I tell her. Me, my husband, the kids. She calls me from the mall to ask for sizes and colors.

I give her the pleasure because these days I'll give her anything, even the gift of buying clothes for us that I know she can't afford.

I need her to see the baby, just in case.

*   *   *

Who am I? I ask myself at the airport magazine stand. Am I *Vogue* or am I *Good Housekeeping*? *Allure* or *Redbook*? I want to be Forever 21, but I'm actually Ann Taylor.

I used to love airports, the enforced idleness between flights. Now we struggle to corral the children. Advantage: early boarding.

*   *   *

I am stunned at what Disneyland is for me now, devastated at the hollowness. I hold her arm as we cross Main Street. I help her with her wallet. I don't let her carry heavy bags. She is more old woman, less mother. I am stunned.

Bewilderment: from a verb that doesn't exist anymore, meaning to lose one's way. In the wild, in the great unknown. My son, my daughter and I awed by how it's all unfolding, we're bewildered.

My son asks Cinderella, *Do you talk?*

Mothers holding and dragging. Cajoling, coaxing, mothers scolding. Children that throw themselves to the ground for desire. The line to the women's bathrooms out the door with children. I rub sunscreen into my son's cheeks. Mothers wearing Tinkerbell sweatshirts.

My mother and I leave my husband with the kids to ride Space Mountain. I love the dark jerks of that ride . . . that my mother loves it too.

The line moves quickly. Can she see okay? I lead her like we're among the halls of a dark hospital. She makes jokes about getting plastic surgery while they do the other surgery. Two for one. She wants me to let go of my worry. I'm reminded of a story: a mother has given her son her heart, she carries him on her back. Something about them falling over her heart that he's dropped, about her worry over his getting hurt from the fall.

Motherhood frays my edges, as does my mother and her body. I long for my husband.

I put my hand over hers and we enter the ride. We don't make a sound. Our bodies slide against each other in the seat. The dry thrill of the ride, the heat of my mother's body.

Fifty dollars for burgers and drinks. The grand struggle of my childhood: insisting that my parents buy me food at Disneyland.

From my mother's notebook: *I'll push her in a silk buggy, the kind from the movies. We'll wear matching sweaters, eat cotton candy. The three hours of the day when all the laundry was done and put away, about as often as a comet came.*

*   *   *

I feel sick after lunch. My stomach churns while I sit on a bench by the bumper cars. *Maybe you're pregnant,* my mother says hopefully. I am dizzy with sick but push through it because it's my son's day. I can barely walk and can barely stand myself for it.

We return to the hotel, where I toss around in the bed with a fever. My mother brings me water and insists I go to the hospital. More child than woman.

From her notebook: *Bread, phone bill. Call daughter and tell her _____ .*

She is all worry. *Hospital, hospital.* I toss around in the bed, my dreams thickened by flu. They're the dreams with yelling in them, with absence. Her refrain: *Just go to see that you're okay.*

Now you know how I feel, Mom.

Did you want anything else? I ask her, because I'm drunk with sick. *Anything else? I have wonderful children,* I say. *What more could I want?* she asks, because she won't take my mother away from me.

I tremble with all the sick I ever was with her.

I can't be sick for long. My husband takes my son to the park. They ride the teacups and come back impatient with me. My son asks me over and over, *Mama you sick?* As if to undo it.

I wobble up onto my elbows to look in his face and vanish the worry. The magician mother.

My mother paces the room, useless. The sick thing can only be for a little while. I have to let it go because of everyone in the room. My mother's worry, my husband's exhaustion, my children need me. I shake it off.

Her trembling and gnarled hand stroking my hair. My son's hand there too.

Ay, Hija, she worries over me. *Hijita,* my little daughter.

I wobble to the bathroom to look at my face in the mirror. My mouth is pulled down a bit by frown lines. Time to return.

They are all outside the door waiting to see how I come out. All these people, dependent and small. I had fought so long against even my own dependence on myself. Got pregnant by accident and then the roll of all this.

How, right before I got pregnant, I had forgotten how to care for myself. I had cast myself out into the world like a streak. Then I became a mother and even more daughter.

The pall of my illness is nearly gone in the morning.

*   *   *

We say good-bye to her. She holds each of our faces in both her hands and stains us with her lipstick. I tease her about her memory and the questions she asks us again and again about our luggage, our flight. I release her from my worry.

I'm the Not Serious Mother. I make jokes about baby Valium, about boarding school. I recycle all my mother's good jokes.

That I'll see her again. That I won't. We're both crying.

I tell my son to say good-bye and he refuses. I push his body close to her and he hits her. What do I say? My son's hurt her and I want to wring his neck. She walks away from us and my son weeps. *I know, I know,* I say to him. My husband puts my son onto his shoulders, and the two of them run to her gate. He tells me they caught her at the last minute, that my son kissed her on the lips, said, *Sorry, Gramma. I love you,* and that my mother nearly collapsed in grief and love.

This trip is the last one before she gets her operation. She's flying to Peru to get the surgery because her health insurance has lapsed. This happened when her memory unfurled out of her. She stopped paying bills, collected them in shoe boxes under her bed. I found them while I was visiting her and tried to make sense of them. Stacks and stacks of bills, most unopened. Her secret life.

I imagine her on the plane and become desperate. So far above us, will she remember who we are? Who she is? Like it's the pull of the earth keeping her herself.

*   *   *

She's packed her bags weeks in advance. She's taking four weeks off work, taken out a loan for the surgery.

I've told everyone about my mother so that they'll hold me up with their good wishes. I interrogate people who know people who've had brain tumors. I need the good stories.

On the day of her surgery I imagine the outcomes, each one of them.

One is dark, and I can barely see it through. I am a child in it.

In the other, she is here and I tend to her for good.

*   *   *

Once, in high school, I went on a date with a boy I met at a dance club. I liked his long hair, his kiss tasting of Vaseline and mint. I didn't dare tell my mother where I was going. The boy lived an hour away, in Santa Cruz. The drive was long and treacherous, over a mountain, winding roads. I imagined what my mother might have thought if she knew where I was. I laughed and shuddered.

The boy took me out to eat and then we walked on the beach. That summer my sister and brother were away with my father in Puerto Rico. It was just my mother and me, alone in the house. I knew her schedule like it was my own, and she would pop into my head during my date. From where I stood on the rocks of the beach I imagined her getting into her car and driving home. I imagined her settling down in front of *Golden Girls*. She was with me.

After the date was over, after our last delicious kiss, the boy told me how to get back to the highway. I was swooning from the kiss, but I also wanted to seem savvy, someone who actually *dated*. I got lost and drove for hours, all over town. Long before cell phones, it didn't occur to me to stop and call my mother. . . . I kept thinking I would find my way. I knew, though—I felt her anxiety growing in that empty house. She calls her sister. She picks up the phone to call my father but doesn't for fear of the blame.

My car fell into a ditch and a man in a tie-dyed union suit pulled me out with his VW bus. I drove down a road the wrong way.

Almost morning, gone long beyond mere trouble.

I found my way to the club where I had met the boy, a landmark, and made my way home from there. I began to think then about how my mother might yell, might hit me. I thought of having to explain to her where I was and not being able to share the giddiness of the kiss because of all her yelling.

When I drove down the street, she was standing on the sidewalk in her robe. Who knows how long she had been standing there? As she saw my car drive up, she turned around and walked back into the house.

Canas verdes.

I came into our darkened house, where she had been alone for hours—imagining what? It's what I spend hours imagining when I want to hurt myself with my motherhood. *To lose your child,* my mother would say, after hearing of a kidnapping on the news. When I bear down on them with all the darkness to disappear it, to cancel it out.

I found her on the couch. She spoke in a voice hoarse from lack of sleep, from waiting. *Do you know what I've been through?* Then she went upstairs to finish dying.

Who knows what waits on the other end of this? Maybe just enormous pain. I remember this night as I wait to hear about her coming out of the other end of this. I feel like she's punishing me for some age-old infraction.

I imagine being pregnant again, one of those women who keeps having babies. The Mother Who Keeps On Keepin' On. More children to help with chores, help me feel young, fulfilled. To love me, to be me.

A carload, a pack, we're cheaper by the dozen.

I once thought I wouldn't be a mother. In my apartment I planned trips to Europe. It felt good to promise mornings to myself, silence.

My mother laughing when I told her about this decision. Merely laughing.

There's no beginning and end to this, her laugh said. It is all part of everything I have done, will do, what I think, what I make. *I'm a mother to begin with.*

The future, the certainty that they will grow older, grow old with me and away from me. That they will experience grief.

That I will have a long life with them.

My son playing video games in his room that smells of armpit and drugstore cologne. My daughter at the counter asking me questions: *How did you and Daddy meet?* The house quiet but for the TV. My daughter losing interest in me when the phone rings. Me in the quiet with nothing to do but think. An interior.

Or it's an apartment. No children yet. Gray outside, rain. Takeout steaming in the kitchen. No one around. Music playing, thrumming the cheap coffee table on which the stereo sits. I smoke a joint and watch the clouds.

I imagine the phone conferences my own children will have about my failing memory.

Granddaughter to Zoila Aurora and Berta Gertrudis, Daughter to Yolanda Noemi, Goddaughter to Olga Victoria, Mother to Sofia Aurora. The ghost-mothers in me. I am Big Mama to my son. His sister is Tiny Mama.

My daughter across the table, surly, tears streaming down her face. A photograph of myself at that age, a quarter of an orange in my mouth, face tilted up, defiantly crying. I want to do something but I can't. *This is just how it is sometimes*, I'll tell her. *It's how it is.*

My son calls me from college. Wispy curls turned to coarse ringlets. I talk to him, I imagine stroking his hair. I get sentimental on the phone and, embarrassed of me, for me, he changes the subject.

My future daughter speaks to me: about desire, its specifics. She's wearing those big, chunky amber rings I was always too shy to wear.

My children ask me about my mother when she was young, because they only knew her when she was old and dying.

My daughter's son, my son's daughter.

My daughter tracing invisible words on her thigh with her fingernail—my own mother's habit.

The memories I'll forget, how my children will remind me.

A photograph of my mother: age ten. You can barely see the girl in her. The hem of her skirt is frayed from running and falling. Her hair is pinned back in tufts. There's a mystery in that smile.

*   *   *

I engage in gluttony and wild behavior in my daydreams, where no one is watching. It's my primary residence. I once had an artist in me. Who knows where she is now? Still inside? I think it may be that my memory is acted upon by the hidden artist. She works to deface what others prize.

I would have liked to have been a dancer. I would have liked to have been a singer.

If only these were my choices: Shoes and a matching purse. Dyed? Or if I had to choose between a house on the ocean or a house in the city. Now those are choices. And now I must decide where to take my tumor. Do I leave it to be handled by the country in which I've lived most of my life, or do I take it back to Peru? There's something poignant about returning to my country to die—or, I hope, to nearly die.

The tumor is like a child in me, or a heartache that feels insistent, physical. I hadn't felt the tumor until the doctor told me about it; now it feels as if it has its own pulse. I've never thought much of my head. I live in my stomach and in my heart. The head is overrated. But now my head flashes bright as a beacon. I follow it, I study and scrutinize.

The doctor and my children worry, but I tell them that I have so much left to think of. They don't realize that, despite the tumor, my brain is well populated with the things I need in order to get through each and every day. I can give you details of about a hundred kisses I've given and received, but maybe not what I had for lunch today. What problem is there in that? My keys? My purse? The name of my daughter's father-in-law? I have beautiful pictures painted in my head—my failings at work pale in light of these masterpieces of memory. My sister tells me when I have appointments and the names of streets. My children remind me to make phone calls about my mortgage. I simply narrate the day in a new way.

When I've forgotten my age, until the mirror. When I forget, my body complies, becomes lithe and strong. My fingers unfurl and become long and straight. Finally I can learn the piano.

I worry myself, but the worry fascinates me. I come upon myself remembering a moment when I was ten years old, the smell of diesel in the air, the buses having just passed by. I wouldn't wash, wouldn't change my clothes. I played football with the boys. The sun going down and it was still warm but the wind was cold. I was inside the air, just me, and it was enough. The smell of my alpaca sweater, the chill of the sweat beneath it. This is enough for me.

I have lived in darkness from time to time. I felt my mother pass through me, into the wind.

Two men I loved when I was young: Enrique, blue-eyed and went to a different school, sang like Elvis; and Jorge. I married Jorge, whom I had befriended out of pity when he was eleven. They say youth is wasted on the young, but I think the body is wasted on the young as well. My daughters, my niece, they worry themselves out of their beauty. They will be sorry for that one day.

When I was thirty-five I saw Charles Aznavour in an airport in Mexico. I told him I had all his records and I loved each one of them—so romantic. He was surrounded by tall, blonde women. Desire so pure it made my skin cold. I hadn't known the body could feel this way. That was enough for me.

When I was a waitress I would often come home with another man's eyes still burning on me. I became only body and legs and skin and mouth, and my husband would know. I can remember it five or six times, like they were holidays. I remember! He said it was like I had become a stranger. He loved my crooked pinkie and that my hair smelled of peaches. Maybe that was all I needed?

Now, when I look at a man, I see all the accompanying trouble, I smell it. Back and forth with desire: better alone than in bad company. Man's body, man's ego, man's machismo.

What the story of my body has been. Important parts long gone: thyroid, uterus, gallbladder. I am composed of absences. The body shifts, the doctor told me, to accommodate emptiness.

Or what I think the story is. This tumor moves me toward something closer to death, but I am reveling in my body in a new way. I touch my own shoulders as a lover might. The tumor pushes against the part of my brain responsible for movement, at least. It turns me into a pulsing and coarse nerve. To feel the world fresh: this is what I try to do with this. That the wind is going to wrap its arms around me, and then the sun.

I see my story as if I were at a precipice, all the rest valley. The tumor squeezes it out. Once, my children were small; now my children have children. Once, I was a young woman preoccupied with the vicissitudes among my sisters and friends in Lima; then I was pushing a baby buggy through six inches of snow in Bronx, New York, USA. Once, I had never had sex; then I became a wife filled with a child.

Hasn't the body been described as a shell? This is how I comfort myself when I think about dying, my head shaved in a different country. My head, an eggshell to be cracked open. My body will crack open, out will come what I've left inside for so long, covered in jelly and blood. Out will come, finally, my real desire.

Source Credits

Page 1. "I think we are on the track of a lost novelist, a suppressed poet." Virginia Woolf, in *A Room of One's Own* (Harcourt Brace and Company, 1991).

Page 6. "In what furnace? In what brain?" William Blake, adapted from "In what furnace was thy brain?" from "The Tyger," in *Songs of Innocence and Experience* (Oxford University Press, 1990).

Page 9. "For my sake and for all our sakes." James Joyce, in *Ulysses* (Random House, 1986).

Page 16. "Muscles better and nerves more." e.e. cummings, from "i like my body when it is with your," in *100 Selected Poems* (Grove Press, 1994).

Page 16. "Who's ever been naked?" Alice Notley, from "Rita, a Red Rose, Hates Her Clothes," in *Disobedience* (Penguin Press, 2001).

Page 22. "What the hell is she building in there?" Tom Waits, adapted from "What's He Building?" in *Mule Variations* (Anti/Epitaph, 2004).

Page 23. "You think your temper is the worst in the world, but mine used to be just like it." Louisa May Alcott, in *Little Women* (Signet Classics, 2004).

Page 24. "Now my belly is as noble as my heart." Gabriela Mistral, from "Poem of the Mothers," in *Poems and Prose Poems* by Gabriela Mistral (Austin: University of Texas Press, 2002).

Page 27. "The person you choose is someone you would feel alright with in life-and-death levels of tripping." Ina May Gaskin, from *Spiritual Midwifery* (Summertown, Tenn.: The Book Publishing Company, 1977).

Page 27. "These were pains one could follow with one's mind." Margaret Mead, in *Blackberry Winter* (New York: Morrow, 1972).

Page 30. "She would bring down the little birds." Robert Duncan, from "My Mother Would Be a Falconress," in *Bending the Bow*. Copyright © 1968 by Robert Duncan. Reprinted by permission of New Directions Publishing.

Page 35. "The breast is a machine that produces milk, and the mouth a machine coupled to it." Gilles Deleuze and Felix Guattari, in *Anti-Oedipus:*

Capitalism and Schizophrenia (London: Continuum Books, 2004).

Page 43. "Boarded the train there's no getting off." Sylvia Plath, in *The Collected Poems*, edited by Ted Hughes (New York: Harper and Row, 1981).

Page 49. "All our progress is an unfolding." Ralph Waldo Emerson, from "Intellect," in *Essays: First Series* (Belknap Press of Harvard University Press, 1987).

Page 51. "I won't be pregnant anymore, and that is where the emptiness begins." Jenny Boully, from "He Wrote in Code," in *One Love Affair* (Brooklyn: Tarpaulin Sky Press, 2006).

Page 68. "Does my fat ass make my fat ass look fat?" Refrigerator magnet.

Page 71. "This is the secret world of the oracle. How can you hope to understand her before you know what she is really like?" J. M. Coetzee, in *Elizabeth Costello* (New York: Viking, 2003).

Page 73. "I want to hold myself to you but you are myself." Rachel Blau DuPlessis, in *Blue Studios: Poetry and Its Cultural Work* (Tuscaloosa: University of Alabama Press, 2006).

Page 78. "A woman is always hampered." Gustave Flaubert, in *Madame Bovary*, translated by Geoffrey Wall (Penguin Classics, 2002).

Page 80. "My mother-in-law's other car is a broom." Bumper sticker.

Page 83. "Motherhood in our present social state is the sign and seal, the means and methods of a woman's bondage; it forges chains of her own flesh and blood; it weaves chords of her own love and instinct." Mona Caird, in *The Daughters of Danaus* (New York: Feminist Press at the City University of New York, 1989).

Page 83. "True liberty is not defined by a relationship between desire and its satisfaction, but by a relationship between thought and action." Simone Weil, in *Oppression and Liberty*, translated by Arthur Wills and John Petrie (London: Routledge and Paul, 1958).

Page 83. "Stronger than all my afterthoughts is my fury." Euripides, in *Medea*, translated by Ian Johnston (Arlington, Vir.: Richer Resources Publications, 2008).

Page 83. "To return to her . . . to repossess and be repossessed by her." Adrienne Rich, in *Of Woman Born: Motherhood as Experience and Institution* (New York: Bantam Books, 1977).

Page 84. "Into the yolk and white of the one shell." William Butler Yeats, from "Among School Children," in *The Tower* (Scribner, 2004).

Page 92. "I'm a mother to begin with." Bernadette Mayer, in *The Desires of Mothers to Please Others in Letters* (Stockbridge, Mass.: Hard Press, 1994).

Acknowledgments

Sections of this book have appeared in *Labor Pains and Birth Stories*, edited by Jessica Powers and published by Catalyst Press, and in *42opus*.

I would like to thank all my friends and family for their support in writing this book. I'd like to thank all who read the book in manuscript form: Nancy Arora, Kristen Buckles, Rachel Haley Himmelheber, and Mark Wunderlich. Special thanks to Evan Lavender-Smith, my Gordon Lish.

About the Author

Formerly a Teaching-Writing Fellow at the University of Iowa, Carmen Giménez Smith is now an assistant professor of creative writing at New Mexico State University, the publisher of Noemi Press, and the editor-in-chief of *Puerto del Sol*. Her first book, *Odalisque in Pieces*, was published by the University of Arizona Press in 2009. She recently co-edited, with Kate Bernheimer, the anthology, *My Mother She Killed Me, My Father He Ate Me*. She lives in Las Cruces, New Mexico, with her husband and their two children.